Michael Sadgrove has been Dean of Durham since 2003. A former Dean of Sheffield and Precentor of Coventry Cathedral, he has also served as a parish priest in north-east England and as a teacher of biblical studies at a theological college. He is the author of *A Picture of Faith* (Kevin Mayhew, 1995). He was born in London in 1950, is married to a psychotherapist and has four adult children.

For Jenny
because it is the gospel of truth and friendship
27 July 2006

THE EIGHT WORDS
OF JESUS

in the Passion According to St John

Michael Sadgrove

First published in Great Britain in 2007

Society for Promoting Christian Knowledge
36 Causton Street
London SW1P 4ST

The author and publisher acknowledge with thanks permission to reproduce
extracts from the following material:
Helen Gardner (trans.), 'The Dream of the Rood', in Helen Gardner (ed.),
The Faber Book of Religious Verse, London: Faber, 1972.
W. H. Vanstone, *Love's Endeavour, Love's Expense: The Response of Being to the
Love of God*, London: Darton, Longman and Todd, 1979.

British Library Cataloguing-in-Publication Data
A catalogue record for this book is available from the British Library

ISBN-13: 978–0–281–05873–0
ISBN-10: 0–281–05873–3

1 3 5 7 9 10 8 6 4 2

Typeset by Kenneth Burnley, Wirral, Cheshire
Printed in Great Britain by Bookmarque

Contents

———◆———

Preface

This book has a prehistory that is explained in the Introduction. The 'Eight Words' first saw the light of day in Good Friday addresses given at two churches appropriately dedicated to St John the Evangelist: at Ranmoor, Sheffield in 1997 and at Edinburgh in 2001. Conversations with some who heard the addresses and others who read the text suggested that there might be a book in this theme.

I wrote this book during a period of sabbatical leave during the spring and summer of 2006. I am very grateful to my colleagues on the Cathedral Chapter and the Bishop's Staff in the Diocese of Durham for releasing me. The Lord Crewe Trust funded a sabbatical pilgrimage to Compostela, an important period of reflection, gestation and prayer in preparation for writing. While much of the preliminary work was done in our home in France, I could not have completed it without the hospitality and help of Joan Williams and the staff of the Cathedral library, nor without a rock-solid alliance with my secretary Barbara Dodd who vigorously defended me from all distractions. I am grateful to them, as I am for the support and encouragement of the team at SPCK.

My wife Jenny was with me both on the journey to Compostela and throughout the journey of writing about the Passion Narrative. Her accompaniment has been a priceless gift. I am completing this book on the day that happens to be the anniversary of the death of one of St John's great interpreters, Bishop Westcott of Durham. More personally, it is also our thirty-second wedding anniversary. So here is an anniversary present.

Michael Sadgrove
Durham Cathedral

Introduction

The seeds of this book were sown more than 40 years ago. As a youngster, I used to sing in the school choral society. One year we performed J. S. Bach's *St John Passion*, his magnificent setting of the Fourth Gospel's account of Jesus' passion and death. It was unforgettable. It played a key part in my coming to Christian faith. I have loved John's Passion Narrative and the music of Bach ever since.

More recently, I attended a remarkable performance of the *St John Passion*. It had been configured for the stage as kind of sacred opera. Although Bach would probably not have approved, the drama of the work lent itself to this experiment. It was good theatre. All the music was sung from memory, and the chorus clearly enjoyed its role as a noisy crowd swirling aggressively round the stage. My abiding memory is how this turbulent energy seemed to highlight the stillness and nobility of Jesus. In particular, his words stood out as if the music cast a halo round them. That prompted me to take a marker and highlight Jesus' sayings in the biblical text of chapters 18 and 19 of St John's Gospel to see whether any insights emerged.

What I found was this. The words of Jesus in the Passion Narrative fall into eight distinct sayings. The last three are his words from the cross. Each of the eight has its own theme, and together they create a clear sequence: the Eight Words of Jesus in St John's Passion Narrative. What is more, these Eight Words stand out from the text with a heightened significance beyond their immediate context.

This ought not to come as a surprise. John's is the Gospel of the Word made flesh. For him, everything Jesus says is charged with meaning. Since the cross is the climax of the story for St John, we would expect him to invest Jesus' words on his way to the cross with great significance. This is what we find, not least in how they constantly refer back to what he has said and done earlier in the Gospel. As the Word goes to his death, the Eight Words stand as his last testament of truth and love addressed to human beings of every place and time. But the passion includes not only this sequence of words. It includes a silence when Jesus refuses to speak in answer to Pilate's question. That silence is as much a 'word' as the other eight. This book might have been called *Eight Words and a Silence.*

This is not to detach the Eight Words artificially from the story in which they belong, nor to fly in the face of critical approaches to the text. My indebtedness to New Testament scholars will be clear from the outset, and I have mentioned those who have particularly influenced my thinking at the end of the book. Because this is not an academic text, I have not rehearsed the scholarly discussion about the origin and interpretation of the Fourth Gospel and its Passion Narrative (the world itself can hardly contain the books that have been written). I don't suppose that most of my interpretations will surprise anyone who knows the Gospel, though I do sometimes take issue with well-known positions on St John, for instance in relation to Pilate's culpability in the crucifixion.

In this book, 'Passion Narrative' means chapters 18 and 19 of St John's Gospel. This raises a problem straight away, for these two chapters can't be separated from those that precede it. The whole Gospel has this seamless quality: everything belongs with everything else. The anointing of Jesus at Bethany, his entry into Jerusalem, the upper room – all are indissolubly part of John's account of the last week of Jesus' life. We can't understand Golgotha without knowing that Jesus has washed his disciples' feet, shared his bread with Judas, spoken of himself as the friend who lays down his life and prayed that his Father will glorify his name in his 'hour'.

It's clear that the complete Passion Narrative begins at chapter 12 (and at the other end of the story takes in at least chapter 20 as

well). Some scholars call this the 'Book of Glory', part two of the
Gospel that began with the 'Book of Signs' in the first 11 chapters.
Genre study of the Gospel suggests that chapters 18 and 19 have
a different literary character from 12 to 17, and possibly a different literary history as well. So I am following Bach in my more
restricted definition of the passion, and will try to show how these
two chapters draw constantly on what has gone before.

'Eight Words' invites comparison with the 'Seven Last Words' of
Jesus from the cross, a traditional theme for addresses at Good
Friday services. Despite a long and honourable history of preaching in this way, I have reservations about it. The Seven Words are
drawn, of course, from all four Gospels. To merge them into a
single 'text' can obscure what is distinctive to each evangelist and
make it difficult to appreciate the subtleties painted into each of
these four portraits of the crucified Jesus. I have always preferred
to preach through one of the four Passion Narratives because
each story develops in its own way with its own emphases, and
provides a distinctive interpretation of the good news of Christ
crucified.

So my theme in this book is St John's Passion Narrative. What I
hope to offer is an extended meditation on the Eight Words. I
want to discover the significance of each saying within his passion
story and, beyond that, his Gospel itself. And I want to suggest
how each saying prompts connections for us to make between the
passion and our own Christian believing, praying and living
today. This is inevitably personal to this particular reader. But I
hope that by reflecting aloud, as it were, others may be encour-
aged to do their own spiritual 'work' on this marvellous text.

The First Word

John 18.4–8

—————►•◄—————

'Whom are you looking for? . . . I am he.
Whom are you looking for? . . . I have told you that I am he.
So if you are looking for me, let these men go.'

The First Word is about our search.

The Passion Narrative of John is a story of treachery, violence, bloodshed and death. Like Virgil, he sings of 'arms and the man'. We have reached the end of the long, slow build-up to the passion in the previous chapters where Jesus is in the upper room with his disciples. Without warning we are pitched straight into a tale of aggression and conflict whose pace barely slackens until the moment of Jesus' death. It begins in a garden, a place normally associated with restfulness and calm. In the first three Gospels, Gethsemane is where Jesus prays and the disciples sleep. Not here. This garden serves only one function for St John: as the theatre of Jesus' swift betrayal and arrest.

The mob bursts in. The garden is dark, for not only is it night-time, but the deeds planned in it are dark too. So the crowd needs lanterns and torches, even though they plan to arrest the Light of the World (9.5).* You might as well hold a tea light up to the sun. And they bring weapons to take him by force, as if strong-arm tactics were needed to restrain the Good Shepherd who lays down his life of his own accord (10.18). It's the first of many ironies in

---

* Throughout this book, where biblical references are given as numerals only, these always refer to John's Gospel.

the Passion Narrative that we shall notice as we journey through it. This one picks up contrasts between light and darkness and between divine and human power that John has drawn from the outset of his book. With understated artistry, John shows how the devices with which mortals intend to tame the Son of God are both Lilliputian and ridiculous.

The scene is set for the first of the Eight Words. It's a question – the first of five Jesus asks in the opening scenes of the passion. 'Whom are you looking for?' It's not the first time Jesus has asked a question like this. His opening words in the Gospel pose a question that is virtually the same. Two disciples have heard John the Baptist speak about Jesus and want to follow him. He turns and asks them: 'What are you looking for?' (1.38). It's not quite the same question as in the garden: *what*, rather than *who*, are you looking for? *What* is more general than *who*, as if the two men, intrigued by the mysterious reference to the Lamb of God, do not yet quite know that it is a *person* they are in fact seeking.

But it's close enough for there to be an echo of that earlier encounter. Yet there's a clear contrast between them. In the first one when everything is fresh and new, it's a question put to people who are looking for him because they want to believe. 'We have found the Anointed One', the longed-for Messiah. In that moment, a question leads to recognition, and the recognition changes lives, the first of many such occasions in John, as we shall see. But here in the garden, it is different. Judas Iscariot has gone out of the upper room into the night (13.30), for by this time he belongs to the place of shadows where disappointment has given birth to doubt, and doubt to hostility, and hostility to hatred. At least, that is one way of reading the career of Judas Iscariot, but we shall come back to him in a later chapter. John specifically mentions Judas as being with the crowd, for it's as much to him specifically as it is to the guards and malcontents that Jesus puts his question. 'Whom are you looking for,' he asks, as if to recall that earlier life-changing meeting, and give Judas a last opportunity to recognize him for who he is.

They answered, 'Jesus of Nazareth – we're looking for him.' Jesus replies, again twice over, 'I am he.' They have found the right person, as if they needed to be told. But there is more to this answer than Jesus' acknowledgement of who he is. It's not simply that Jesus confirms his identity: more that in his reply, he goes to the very root of his identity. Most English translations don't help here. In Greek it is *ego eimi*, simply 'I am.' Everyone who has read through St John up to this point will recognize the resonances of those two majestic words, and recall the great procession of declarations they have introduced during the course of the Gospel: 'I am the Bread of Life'; 'I am the true Vine'; 'I am the Light of the World'; 'I am the Way, the Truth and the Life'; 'I am the Good Shepherd', 'I am the resurrection and the life.' It's not too much to say that 'I am' is one of the central leitmotifs of St John.

An episode earlier in the Gospel makes it clear what Jesus' meaning is. John organizes the central section of his book around the sharp debates and controversies Jesus generates through his words and actions. In one of these, he is challenged by the Pharisees to account for himself. A heated argument turns to his, and their, relationship with Abraham, whom they all acknowledge as their father in the faith. Events reach an ugly climax when Jesus claims that Abraham looked forward to his own coming: 'your ancestor Abraham rejoiced that he would see my day; he saw it and was glad'. 'Have you seen Abraham?' they reply scornfully, by now convinced that Jesus is mad or very bad. He replies: 'Very truly I tell you, before Abraham was, I am' (8.58): *ego eimi*, words calculated to offend and infuriate, so much so that he narrowly escapes being stoned to death. It is a foreshadowing of the passion, and a clue as to the reasons for it.

Every Jewish reader of the Fourth Gospel would understand the origin of those two words in the Hebrew Bible. At the beginning of Israel's history, the Hebrews are enslaved in Egypt, crying out for deliverance. Moses encounters God in an awe-inspiring epiphany at the burning bush. God charges him to take the message of liberation to his people. Full of foreboding, he asks by what name he is to speak to them of God. Out of the bush calls the divine voice, mysterious, enigmatic. 'I AM WHO I AM,' it says; 'Thus you shall say to the Israelites, "I AM has sent me to you"' (Exodus 3.1–15).

This is the origin of the name YHWH by which the Hebrew Bible knows the God of Israel. The precise meaning defies translation or explanation, for the name of God is the profoundest mystery at the heart of the universe. Strictly speaking it is 'ineffable' – it is too holy to be spoken by mortals, which is why Jewish readers of the Hebrew text replace it with the reverent title *Adonai*, 'The LORD', a tradition followed in most English versions. But the divine name seems to imply that Israel's God YHWH is the origin and ground of all being and becoming; all existence, all life, all activity, all purpose rests on his creating, sustaining power. By disclosing himself in this way, God draws Moses and the people of Israel right into the heart of the mystery of his own being.

So when Jesus says, 'before Abraham was, I am', his meaning is not lost on the Jewish teachers and leaders. Their fury lies in his blasphemous claim to embody the presence of 'I AM', the living God. In the garden at night-time, the crowd's reaction to Jesus' *ego eimi* is similar. They fall back in astonishment that a man should dare to take to himself the sacred name of God. Even in his arrest, John's Jesus does not lose the power to amaze and shock.

*   *   *

'Whom do you seek?' The question is universal to the human race. The passion story is about all that we are looking and longing for, whether we realize it or not. The gospel answers our long search for meaning in a world that often seems meaningless and perplexing. It says there is a point of light to guide us as we stumble around the garden in the darkness, an apt image of our confusion. It bears witness to truth, as Jesus will say later on, in a world of falsehood and lies. It invites us to see how, even in places of hopelessness, Jesus stands majestic and welcoming and says to us, whoever we are, 'I am the one you have been looking for.'

God's disclosure to Moses at the burning bush, and later on to the Hebrews in the desert, sensitized Israel to the Holy One in their midst. He had become their God and made them his people, and taught them to read the whole of life by the light of this revelation of 'the holy'. All of the law and the prophets flow directly out of it, for the Hebrew scriptures are shot through with a sense of the 'presence' of the divine. In the same way, the 'I AM' of the Passion Narrative brings the invitation to see our existence as shaped by God's presence in the world as his crucified Son. Bishop John Taylor's experience of African religion gave him a particular feeling for 'the holy' both in other human beings and in the natural order. He looked for a purified vision among those who had begun to glimpse something of this divine 'presence' around them and within. He wrote about

> the listening, responsive, agonising receptivity of the prophet and the poet. For it is impossible to be open and sensitive in one direction without being open to all. If a man would open his heart toward his fellow he must keep it open to all other comers – to the stranger, to the dead, to the enchanting and awful presences of nature, to powers of beauty and terror, to the pain and anxiety of men, to the menace and catastrophe of our time, and to the overwhelming presence of God . . . To present oneself to God means to expose yourself, in an intense and vulnerable awareness, not only to him but to all that is. And this is what, apart from Christ, we dare not do. Presence is too much for us to face.   (Taylor, 1963, pp. 191–2)

This quality of 'intense and vulnerable awareness' is the first gift of a living faith. If we were to ask John what shape this has for those who follow Jesus, he would answer unhesitatingly that it's to the cross that we need to look. For it is there that human beings are brought into a new relationship with God and with one another, and where truth is displayed before the world. To look at the cross is to encounter God's 'I AM' present to the whole of creation as love poured out. And that is to be sensitized to 'the love that moves the sun and the stars', as Dante so memorably put it at the end of *The Divine Comedy*. All this is to anticipate what the Passion Narrative will unfold. But if we speak about this awareness that the cross gives us as a kind of 'transfigured vision', we are perhaps close to John's mind. The invitation in the garden, as so often in St John's Gospel, is to search and to see in a new way. The crowd is blind to it, but John hopes that we, his readers, will not be.

I recently drove with my wife along the medieval pilgrimage route from central France to Santiago de Compostela. We wanted to follow the tracks of the millions who have travelled the thousand miles of the 'Camino' to the shrine of St James the Great in the far north-western corner of Spain. We met pilgrims as we stopped on the way to visit and pray in churches and chapels, and passed hundreds more along the road, some walking, some cycling, a few on horseback, all sporting the *coquille* or scallop shell, symbol of St James the Great and of the pilgrimage to his shrine. It was moving to see this great human procession spread out along northern Spain, a tide of purposeful travel embracing, we found, just about every human motivation and aspiration possible. A German woman who had suffered from a serious illness had vowed to walk to Compostela if she recovered. A young Australian was looking for a change of pace from her demanding job in a caring profession. Two Americans were walking for the seventh time because the Camino was 'in their blood'. An elderly French married couple, fervent Catholics, were looking for spiritual renewal and growth. One study of the pilgrimage analyses people's motives for making the pilgrimage. Some want to deal with life crises – unemployment, divorce or bereavement – by taking a long journey to regain a perspective on life. Some have consciously religious reasons for making the pilgrimage. Some want to make a counter-cultural statement by making a slow and self-powered journey in an age of rapid and polluting transportation (Frey, 1999).

I doubt if most of those walking the Camino knew precisely

what to expect at the end of it, and how the pilgrimage would turn out to have affected their lives. In the Middle Ages, the point of pilgrimage was well understood: you made a penitent journey to the saint's relics to gain remission of sins. Today there are no commonly agreed reasons for doing it. Postmodern pilgrimage is about whatever comes out of your own 'story'. Everyone's journey has equal validity, and you don't necessarily expect your experience to be the same as anyone else's.

But the extraordinary revival of the popularity of pilgrimage in recent decades may say something important about the contemporary world and the spiritual mood of our time. It's rash to generalize. But maybe the threats we face today, such as the environmental crisis, terrorism and conflict, global poverty, the deadening effects of consumerism, contribute to a profound malaise among people who stop to think about the values they live by. Pilgrimage can be a symbol of wanting to live more responsibly, with a heightened sense of awareness. Socrates said that 'the unreflected life is not worth living'. Our humanity is denied if we close the door on the search for meaning and authenticity. All this is not a long way from the religious quest itself and from Jesus' two Johannine questions: first '*What* are you looking for?' and then '*Whom*?' We won't find the answer until we are prepared to travel mentally and spiritually, and make the life-changing journey into God.

*   *   *

To know that we have embarked on this journey of awareness is a mark of wisdom, or, as we might call it, 'spiritual intelligence'. One of its outcomes is to realize the extent to which we are not our own, but are always caught up in forces over which we have little or no control. These forces are the social, cultural and geopolitical facts that govern much of our existence, and in the face of them we can feel increasingly impotent and angry. We tend to think of these forces as a feature of our own age, and perhaps the degree to which we are *conscious* of them is such a feature, though I doubt if any of them – even consumerism and the pursuit of pleasure – are entirely new: eighth-century Israel and the later centuries of the Roman empire are evidence of that.

The 'crowd' can perhaps be the Passion Narrative's symbol of these oppressive forces. The power of the crowd and its hold over individuals was a theme that fascinated the nineteenth-century Danish philosopher and theologian Søren Kierkegaard. He identified the frightening ease with which people lose touch with themselves, lose themselves in the pack and start behaving in ways that are unpredictable, irrational or even evil. He wrote that 'one can only say of people *en masse* that they know not what they do . . . A demon is called up over whom no individual has any power' (Kierkegaard, 1973, p. 261). He never tired of pointing out that it takes huge courage for someone to emerge from the hiding place the crowd provides and become an individual making decisions on the basis of conscience and belief.

The power of 'the crowd' plays a large part in John's Passion Narrative; indeed it's the engine that drives much of the narrative along. It is the crowd that secures Jesus' arrest, screams for Jesus' crucifixion, plays into Pilate's fear of the emperor's displeasure, convinces itself that its real king is Caesar and not God, taunts the Son of God and clamours for the release of a murderer. The turbulent atmosphere, electric with pent-up rage, acts as a foil for the majestic figure of Jesus as he moves through the story towards his death. In Bach's *St John Passion*, the energetic choruses that portray the crowd's violent, conflicted emotions are among the most memorable movements of that great work.

All this is foreshadowed when the mob bursts into the garden. So we must not miss the symbolism of Jesus' first question being addressed to the crowd who have come to arrest him. We can see him challenging not only the *mores* of the mob collectively but the minds of the individuals who make it up. His challenge is to anyone who has the courage to emerge from their double concealment in a big crowd and a deep darkness. Whom do you seek? Who will take up the cause of Jesus? Who will take issue with the herd and acknowledge that their search is not for someone to arrest so much as someone to follow and love? This is an accurate picture of our condition in the twenty-first century. The issue for those who covet 'spiritual intelligence' is how we are going to be called out of the global 'crowd' and the pressures that control us so that we can become individuals who are truly committed to our search, aware of who and what alone makes for creative, authentic living.

It is the task of religion to honour that search and name it. The search, important though it is, can never be enough on its own – this is St John's point. Despite the aphorism about travelling hopefully, pilgrimage is always about arrival as well as the journey. Human beings can only be made whole as they come to recognize the divine 'I AM' embodied in the person of Jesus. And as the story will go on to tell, there is one place of recognition above all else where the nature of Jesus is fully disclosed to the entire world. That is Golgotha, the place of crucifixion where the last words, 'It is accomplished!' answers for all time the first words, 'Whom are you looking for?' It is not enough, says St John, that we follow the man who teaches about love and performs great signs. It is Jesus the crucified Son of God he wants us to recognize and know.

*   *   *

This first saying of Jesus does not stop with his 'I AM.' He goes on to refer to those with him in the garden. 'I told you that I am he. So if you are looking for me, let these men go.' St John adds a note of explanation: 'This was to fulfil the word that he had spoken, "I did not lose a single one of those whom you gave me".' These explanatory comments, so characteristic of John, are scattered right across the Passion Narrative. They are marks of his insistence that what is happening to Jesus is not a matter of chance. This apparent tragedy is taking place in a way that is planned and purposeful. Far from being the helpless victim of circumstances, Jesus remains in control of his own destiny. It was all known about long before. So John reinforces the point by showing how the passion fulfils the Hebrew scriptures, or as here, something Jesus has already said in his ministry.

'Let these men go' is meant to be read at different levels: St John is the New Testament's master when it comes to multiple meanings. Most obviously, Jesus is protecting his disciples from being caught up in and destroyed by the events that will lead to his death. The angry crowd are looking for him, not them: it is *his* controversy, not theirs, at least for now. So for a time the disciples recede into the background. The high priest will ask Jesus about them (18.19), but in their absence; for Peter and 'another disciple' are outside at the time and the others are nowhere to be seen. Soon Peter drops out of the story too, and this leaves only that other disciple, the one 'whom Jesus loved', who is present with the women at the cross.

St John sees this as a fulfilment of words spoken earlier by Jesus. In his prayer before the passion, Jesus hands over to the protection of his Father those 'whom he has given him'. As he prays for his disciples, this infant community of love so precious yet so precarious, he tells how he has cared for them in his ministry: 'While I was with them, I protected them in your name . . . I guarded them, and not one of them was lost except the one destined to be lost, so that the scripture might be fulfilled' (17.12). And this in turn draws on a saying earlier in the Gospel: 'this is the will of him who sent me, that I should lose nothing of all that he has given me, but raise it up on the last day' (6.39). 'Gather up the fragments', says Jesus after he has fed the crowd, 'so that nothing may be lost' (6.12).

John's image is of the church being protected against the assaults of evil. He is probably writing at a time when Christians were enduring persecution at the hands of the Romans. His theme is that his readers do not need to be afraid despite the threats. Suffering and death may await some of them as they awaited Jesus; but nothing is ever wasted, not the tiniest spark of faith and love, for all that most of the disciples have proved and will prove again to be very flawed followers of Jesus. It is harder for us in the West to hear in this story the overtones of a young church at risk of destruction, though many Christians in other parts of the world today do read the Fourth Gospel out of the same experience of hostile pressure. For fragile communities of faith past and present, the promise that everything is ultimately gathered up in Christ is infinitely reassuring.

'Let these men go' marks a watershed in the Fourth Gospel. Up to now, those whom God has 'given' Jesus to be with him in his ministry have remained close to him in a community of the deepest love and intimacy. But the time has come for separation and departure. Jesus has prepared them for this moment when he must 'go away' to the place where they cannot come (13.33ff.). Despite their forebodings, this is not abandonment. It is their salvation. They will not be left by themselves: Jesus has underlined this again and again in the upper room. Yet the work that has to be done can be done only by him. He must face suffering and death alone. It is another great theme of St John that deliverance is won without the help of anyone else. 'I looked, but there was no helper,' says the conqueror in the prophet's vision; 'so my own arm brought me victory' (Isaiah 63.5). As the hymn says, 'Thou must save, and thou alone.'

The image of the lonely figure of Jesus being bound in the darkness of the garden is one of the most poignant in the story. In St Mark, the garden is where the disciples desert Jesus and run away (Mark 14.50). But in St John they leave because he tells them to. And straight away one of the disciples, Peter (of course), does the exact opposite. Instead of leaving the garden he draws his sword to protect his master, and this immediately after Jesus has spoken about how the role of protector is his alone! This reaction calls forth the Second Word of Jesus, his rebuke to Peter that we shall come to in the next chapter.

Peter typifies an instinct within us, and it is entirely understandable, that refuses to leave Jesus alone and insists on 'defending' him. I am thinking of the various pressures that the church in our society is under and that risk compromising its effectiveness, if not its existence. Externally, a powerful secularism and the increasing confidence of other faith communities are the context of Christian life and mission in the twenty-first century.

Internally, the voices of division between Christians are becoming more strident by the day: church order, sexual relations, abortion, euthanasia, the place of women in the church, and (because these controversies are symptoms of the deeper theological issue) the nature of authority and the role of scripture.

In this difficult environment, the cry often goes up that we must 'defend Christ' against the threats that would weaken the church's faith and undermine its mission. This is a dangerous tactic because it forces faith into a polarized, absolutist mode where there is no real meeting and no understanding of how Christian thinking and living takes place within often radically different contexts. George Carey has said that this defensive posture cannot be right. What we are called to do is not to 'defend' Christ, but something much harder, which is faithfully to bear witness to him. 'Witness' is a key word in St John, as we shall see. To be a good witness requires that we are properly placed both to see and to tell. This needs distance as well as closeness. When Jesus says to the crowd 'I AM', he invokes a strand in Israel's tradition in which humans were commanded to keep their distance from the awesome flame of God's presence. This was holy ground where mortals ventured at their peril. The burning bush needed no defending – but with a wayward, doubting Israel to persuade, it *did* need witnessing to. John is saying that it's the same on the road to the cross.

Seeking Jesus and letting go of him are linked in this First Word. Symbolically, this is a way of saying that the disciples have to 'go their way' if humanity is going to search after Jesus and find him. The world's salvation depends on their carrying the message of Christ crucified and risen. This is a point for a 'mission-shaped church' to ponder. If we are going to be effective evangelists, defensiveness is the least desirable and attractive stance to adopt. What is needed is to point to Jesus in a spirit of humility, openness and generosity towards those who do not (yet) see him as we do.

And when we do this, we open up the possibility that others can begin to enter into the experience of the men and women John writes so lovingly about in his Gospel, such as Nicodemus, the woman of Samaria, the man born blind, Mary, Martha and Lazarus. These all stumble into Jesus and are set on the path towards the goal of their search. To meet Jesus is to discover how unformed longings and unexpressed hopes are met and given shape. At first, his *ego eimi* in the dark garden of our search is as strange to us as it was to the crowd who fell to the ground. Yet his word confirms that he is the one we have been looking for all along. He calls us to throw away our lanterns, torches and weapons, everything with which we defend ourselves and ward off his loving approach. He invites us to say 'Yes' to his kingship, and taste the truth that sets us free – like the Hebrews whom Moses told of his meeting with God and smelled freedom in the air.

*   *   *

Once more in St John's Gospel Jesus asks the question, 'Whom are you looking for?' That happens in another garden, this time not at night but in the early morning. A woman comes to the tomb of the man she loves and finds it empty. Someone she takes to be the gardener puts to her that question: 'Who are you looking for?' And when he calls her by her Hebrew name *Mariam*, she realizes with a rush of joy who he is. This divine Gardener is the risen One who has inaugurated the new creation on the first day of the week. It is another of John's unforgettable recognition scenes, one of the greatest – not simply in the Bible but in all of literature.

In the primeval history in Genesis, God came looking for Adam and Eve in the garden of Eden with his question, 'Where are you?' Then, the man and the woman hid from him. In Gethsemane, Jesus' question is addressed to people who also are hiding in the darkness, unwilling to face the light of truth. But on Easter Day the time for concealment is over. This last time that Jesus puts his question, it's to a woman who is hoping against hope. We see resurrection faith being born in her. St John tells his story 'so that you may believe'. This is where we find and follow the One who seeks us out and calls us by name – and as we find him, we find our own true selves again.

The Second Word

John 18.11

'Put your sword back into its sheath.
Am I not to drink the cup that the Father has given me?'

The Second Word is about destiny.

Of the Eight Words in St John's Passion Narrative, only two are
directly addressed to people who are personally close to Jesus. One
is for Peter, and the other for his mother and the beloved disciple.
But there is a sharp contrast between them. The Sixth Word,
where he bequeaths his mother to the care of his disciple, is gentle
and endearing. But this Second Word is a sharp rebuke. Peter has
drawn his sword and lashed out at the high priest's slave Malchus,
hacking off his right ear (John is very specific about the details of
this incident, though it is only in Luke's Gospel that Jesus turns to
heal the injured man). Jesus reprimands him. 'Put your sword
back into its sheath.' And this for doing what anyone would
instinctively do: defend your friend against those about to do him
harm.

We should not judge Peter too harshly. In the confusion of
struggle and conflict, most people find themselves reacting by
instinct rather than responding with judgement. The annals of
war are littered with stories of civilians, decent people, who were
wrong-footed by what they saw and experienced: in the clear light
of day they would never have dreamed of injuring or killing a
fellow human being. We are right to say when we hear about some
atrocity or other in a place where life is cheap that in those circumstances we might have been capable of anything. Violence

begets violence. If ever there was a man in the Gospels who was bound to be caught up in the spiral of retaliation, it would be the headstrong, impetuous Peter. True to form, he reacts by instinct. But at least it is a loyal, faithful instinct.

In this arena where the stark choice is fight or flight, Jesus' intervention arrests the cycle of violence and bloodshed before it can escalate further. 'Put your sword back into its sheath'; and with it, the machismo, the urge to dominate which not for the first time threatens to be Peter's undoing. Jesus' message is that violence is not to be the way; at least, not violence done on his behalf. It's true that there is a violence Jesus does not resist in the Gospel, but it is the violence *done to* him by others, not taking up arms in his defence. The passion of Jesus is the renunciation of force. He is *done to*, but will not retaliate in kind. He has accepted the vocation of the victim, for he is the Lamb of God who dies to take away the sins of the world; he is the Son of Man lifted up so that all may come to him; he is the Good Shepherd who sacrifices himself for those he cares for; he is the friend whose greater love leads to the laying down of his own life. These powerful Johannine images of self-offering stand in the strongest possible contrast to how Peter would resolve matters in the garden that night.

In the Cathedral of Santiago there is a baroque sculpture of St James on horseback brandishing a sword, triumphant for Christendom and for Spain. In the Middle Ages, the Compostela pilgrimage was a highly political act, for it was the inspiration at the heart of the *Reconquista*, the long, slow expulsion from Spain of Islam that began in the eighth century and was only completed in the fifteenth. You come across this image of *Santiago Matamoros*, James the Moor-slayer, all over Spain. In his hour of victory, James is crushing underfoot hapless Muslims. True to his biblical nickname 'son of thunder', there is not a trace of sympathy for the victim in his face, not a hint of compassion: it is war to the death. It is disconcerting to get so close to it – there is no distance to lend, if not enchantment, at least decency. In an age of inter-faith sensitivities, the cathedral authorities have the good sense to mask the lower part of the sculpture with large flower arrangements so that you can only glimpse what is underneath. But it is thought-provoking to realize that a pilgrimage of discipleship and renewal turns out to carry so many associations with violence and conflict.

This comes closer to home. As I gaze out on the walls of Durham Cathedral rising like a huge yellow sandstone cliff only yards from our kitchen window, I often think about the paradox of this extraordinarily beautiful place where I have the privilege of working. To me and to millions of people across the world, the cathedral is not only the epitome of Romanesque architecture, one of the world's great masterpieces. It is also, like Compostela, a place of pilgrimage, the shrine of St Cuthbert, a focus of human search and divine transformation. People say that the building has a remarkable quality about it that can only be expressed in the language of the 'spiritual', a sacrament in stone. For many people it's a cathedral that moves them deeply.

Of course I don't argue with that: it's the same for me. Yet the historical fact is that it was built by the Normans as a symbol of their power over the recently conquered Saxons, whom in the north they treated with particular cruelty. In today's language, the Northumbrians were subjected to nothing less than ethnic cleansing. Cuthbert, the humble saint of Lindisfarne around whose shrine the Normans erected the grandest of their cathedrals, was roundly appropriated to a new cause, which was to serve the aims of William the Conqueror in making good his successes in England. It is a strange alliance of simplicity and slaughter. In later centuries, Cuthbert's banner was unfurled on the battlefield to secure victory over the Scots. These episodes are not unique: similar stories could be told the length and breadth of Europe.

'Sword and crown betray his trust,' says the hymn. But our Christian history, like that of so many other religious faiths, shows how reliant we have been on the sword. The events in the garden on Maundy Thursday foreshadow precisely this tendency. I doubt whether Christianity has climbed clear enough of this all-too-human 'Petrine' way of being to put its sword back in its sheath quite yet. To underline the point, Jesus returns to the issue of violence in the Fourth Word when he explains his kingship to Pilate: 'if my kingship were from this world, my servants would be fighting'. We shall come back to it then.

*   *   *

To be *passive*, literally, means the same thing as to experience *passion*; that is, to suffer. When you are passive, things are done *to* you: you have relinquished the will or the power to act on your own behalf. You have become a victim. But we need to take care how we use this kind of language in relation to Jesus in the Fourth Gospel. St John is clear that, on the way to the cross, Jesus is far from being 'passive' in the sense that he is not responsible for what happens to him. Throughout the Gospel he declares that 'his hour' has not yet come. What this means becomes progressively clearer as the Gospel unfolds. It also becomes clear that only when that time has arrived will anyone be able to touch him.

Throughout the Gospel Jesus waits for the time to be fulfilled. Nothing happens to him by chance. Everything is known before it happens and must take place as intended: it was for this that he came into the world. So when Jesus enters the last week of his life, John emphasizes that the waiting is now over. Jesus prays in distress: 'Now my soul is troubled. And what should I say – "Father, save me from this hour"? No, it is for this reason that I have come to this hour' (12.27). John introduces the upper room sequence (chapters 13 to 17) by telling us that 'Jesus knew that his hour had come to depart from this world and go to the Father'. We now know what this 'hour' is that we have been waiting for all this time. It is his passion when Jesus is 'lifted up' in death. And we need to understand how for John the cross is a decisive act of sovereignty, not the capitulation of an impotent victim. 'No one takes it [my life] from me, but I lay it down of my own accord. I have power to lay it down, and I have power to take it up again' (10.18). Jesus goes on to say, 'I have received this command from my Father.'

'Power' here is *exousia*, more 'authority' than merely raw force (which is *dynamis*). To lay down his life is *required* of him because of who he is. It carries the authority of God himself.

That is what lies behind the second part of this Word: 'Am I not to drink the cup my Father has given me?' In the Hebrew Bible, the 'cup' of God is an image of suffering and destiny. In one of the laments uttered at a time when it seemed that God had rejected his own people, the psalmist complains that 'you have made your people to suffer hard things; you have given us wine to drink that made us reel' (Psalms 60.3). A victory song draws on the same imagery, ascribing the suffering of the wicked to God's judgement: 'In the hand of the LORD there is a cup with foaming wine, well-mixed; he will pour a draught from it, and all the wicked of the earth shall drain it down to the dregs' (Psalms 75.7–8). In one of the prophets, salvation means having this cup taken away: 'See, I have taken from your hand the cup of staggering; you shall drink no more from the bowl of my wrath' (Isaiah 51.22). In the other Gospels Jesus prays in Gethsemane that the bitter cup may pass from him.

In drinking this cup held out to him by God, Jesus is embracing not simply his own vocation but the entire destiny of his people. This is not a new theme in St John. From the outset he has presented Jesus as the embodiment of what the people of Israel were called be. Their vocation had been given to them and set out in the law and the prophets. They were to be the seed of Abraham through whom the world would find blessing. They were to be a light to the nations. They were to be the obedient son of God and the suffering servant of the Lord. At the outset of the Gospel Jesus recognizes in Nathanael 'an Israelite in whom there is no deceit' (1.47). But how much more is this true of Jesus himself, this new Moses who leads his people to freedom. So this true Israelite goes willingly into suffering and exile. There, his obedience will win the victory that Israel through her perennial failures of vision and understanding consistently failed to achieve.

Tom Wright puts it like this:

At the heart of Jesus' symbolic actions, and his retelling of Israel's story, there was a great deal more than political pragmatism, revolutionary daring, or the desire for a martyr's glory. There was a deeply theological analysis of Israel, the world, and his own role in relation to both. There was a deep sense of vocation and trust in Israel's god, whom he believed of course to be God. There was the unshakeable belief . . . that if he went this route, if he fought this battle, the long night of Israel's exile would be over at last, and the new day for Israel and the world would really dawn once and for all. He himself would be vindicated . . . and Israel's destiny, to save the world, would thereby be accomplished.   (Wright, 1996, pp. 609–10)

Not only does Jesus accept this vocation, he is *thirsty* for it, as we shall see when we come to the Seventh Word. Only then will he utter the last and greatest Word of all, which is to announce that his destiny is realized and his vocation complete.

*   *   *

How does this 'cup' of Jesus, and the cross it points to, shape our search for 'spiritual intelligence'? What is Christianity according to St John?

He could give several answers. One of them would draw on Jesus' prayer before his passion: 'and this is eternal life, that they may know you, the only true God, and Jesus Christ whom you have sent' (17.3). Eternal life does not mean, or does not principally mean, 'life after death'. It's John's phrase for a transformed way of living in the present where everything is lit up by the Spirit of the risen Jesus. 'Everything' means our personal life, our life-in-relationships and our life-in-society. The key is Jesus himself and how he embodies what it means to be human. In John's Gospel he models not only the man of prayer and scripture, wisdom, poise and judgement who lives the well-ordered life. He is also the man whose signs demonstrate his passionate care for other human beings; who inaugurates a society of relationships informed by love; and who washes feet because, in the life of this renewed humanity, the fundamental stance of one human being toward another is humility. Above all, he accepts his destiny, drinks the cup held out to him and lays down his life. For John, the suffering Jesus is at the centre of his vision of the transformed life.

On its release in 2004, Mel Gibson's film *The Passion of the Christ* achieved what every director covets: huge publicity. Not long after its DVD release, my youngest daughter suggested we pass a rainy half-term afternoon watching it. I had misgivings, having read some of the reviews. Peter Bradshaw, the *Guardian*'s film critic, wrote scathingly about 'Gibson's foolish and shallow film': 'Is it too much to ask where the spiritual dimension has disappeared to? Where is the message of love, and hope? Where is the compelling poetry of moral grace? Does all of it have to be swept away in a tsunami of fake gore?' (*Guardian*, 26 March 2004). Theologians joined in, criticizing the film's 'gratuitous' violence, its alleged anti-Semitism in attaching blame to the Jews for the crucifixion, and its uncritical merging of the passion accounts into a single narrative (Corley and Webb, 2004). On the other hand, there was the predictable hype from traditionalist Christians of both a Catholic and Protestant hue. Churches organized evangelistic visits to the cinema. Pope John Paul is supposed to have commented of the film, 'It is as it was' – but if he didn't, others certainly said as much. Neither the enthusiasm nor the criticism seemed encouraging at the time.

A few minutes into the film, I was surprised to have to conclude that it did need to be taken seriously after all. The performances and direction were commendable. The dialogue in Aramaic and Latin throughout (with subtitles!) created a sense of antiquity and remoteness from our time that was exactly right. It is not a perfect film, by any means. But it is as a *film* that it has to be judged, not as history or theology or evangelistic message. The focus on the pain and suffering of Jesus was hard to watch, but it was a forcible reminder of the cruelty of the ancient world. Some of the criticism of the film's violence suggested to me that the fault lay not in the screen but in ourselves, in our wish for a passion detached from its awful ancient context, cleaned up to make it watchable. René Girard, whose writings on violence in religious contexts have deeply influenced many theologians, says that 'the invisible but supreme force that manipulates all of these critics without their realizing it' can only be the passion itself (Girard, 2004).

As I tried to locate the film in some identifiable tradition, I realized that it came straight out of the Western medieval world with its intense devotion to the suffering Christ. He is vividly depicted in his agony in thousands of paintings, sculptures, hymns and poems. I had seen something comparable to it in great art. It was in Colmar in Alsace, where I saw a painting that I knew I would never forget. It's the terrible but magnificent crucifixion by Matthias Grünewald from the early sixteenth century known as the Isenheim Altarpiece. It stops you in your tracks, so extreme is its depiction of the agony of the Son of God. His body is pulled apart by the pain, his flesh furrowed with the marks of his abuse. At the foot of the cross is a lamb whose throat has been slit, its blood pouring into a chalice. The painting was commissioned for a monastic hospital, a sign of Christ suffering in and with human beings. As Richard Harries puts it, this Christ 'expresses, in the most brutally realistic way, the conviction that God himself in Christ experiences the violence of human life, of which people in the sixteenth century and the twenty-first century were and are so conscious' (Harries, 2004, p. 95).

It is picked up in the twentieth century by Graham Sutherland in his tormented figure at the foot of his great tapestry of 'Christ in Glory' in Coventry Cathedral. Comparing it to Grünewald's painting, I have said elsewhere that 'Sutherland's tapestry is, if anything, even bleaker' (Sadgrove, 1995, p. 98). The Passion Play at Oberammergau draws on the same tradition. So indeed does the communion service of the Book of Common Prayer, where the focus is so concentrated on the passion and death of Christ that the resurrection seems present only by implication. In poetry,

the Anglo-Saxon 'Dream of the Rood' imagines the cross itself
remembering what it was like to carry the Son of God:

> I was wet with teeming blood,
> Streaming from the warrior's side when he sent forth his spirit.
> High upon that hill helpless I suffered
> Long hours of torment; I saw the Lord of Hosts
> Outstretched in agony; all-embracing darkness
> Covered with thick clouds the corpse of the World's Ruler;
> The bright day was darkened by a deep shadow,
> All its colours clouded; the whole creation wept,
> Keened for its King's fall; Christ was on the Rood.
>
> (Gardner, 1972, p. 26)

And from the thirteenth century comes the *Stabat Mater Dolorosa*,
one of the greatest of medieval Latin hymns:

> At the Cross her station keeping,
> stood the mournful Mother weeping,
> close to Jesus to the last.
>
> Bruised, derided, cursed, defiled,
> she beheld her tender Child
> all with awful scourges rent.

We are invited to stand with Mary at the cross and contemplate
the suffering of her son. The poem does this with a painful intensity that at times seems almost unbearable:

> Holy Mother! pierce me through,
> in my heart each wound renew
> of my Saviour crucified:
>
> Let me share with thee His pain,
> who for all my sins was slain,
> who for me in torments died.

It would be a mistake to think that this kind of spirituality is no more than an indulgence in pain for its own sake. It is the redemptive significance of the suffering of God's Son that is the point. Ellen Ross, in a thoughtful exploration of how the image of the suffering Jesus was understood in late medieval England, believes that at the heart of this tradition is the belief that 'suffering manifested divine presence and at times, erased the boundaries between the Divine and human in empowering women and men to become agents of God in the world'. She suggests that 'in our own time . . . when the AIDS crisis and anxiety about bodies . . . shape the cultural discourse of our age, we may better understand our own culture by reflecting on a period in which the fascination with blood and bodies had a very different cultural meaning' (Ross, 1997, p. 138).

Where did this all come from? The answer has to be, despite the elaboration and embellishments, from the four Gospels themselves. Obviously imaginative interpretation plays a part in this: the Gospels are more reticent in the way they portray Jesus' sufferings than some of their commentators in art, music and liturgy have been. But we need to remember how large a proportion of all four Gospels is given to the events of passion week. In St John's case, no less than one-third of the Gospel directly concerns the last seven days of Jesus' life, a concentration of focus that shows just how central the passion was to the early church's proclamation of the Gospel. The old tag that the four Gospels are 'Passion Narratives with introductions' is especially true in St John's case.

So how ought the passion to shape our spirituality? We shall come back again and again to this question, for it's a basic theme of this book. But we must begin somewhere. As we hear Jesus speak about the cup he must drink, and meditate on the cross as the primary and precious symbol of our faith, there is one response that must come before everything else. That is to place ourselves before the cross as thankful recipients of the priceless gift that is our liberation from slavery, our homecoming from exile, our light in darkness and our life in death.

We need to develop a spirituality of gratitude. The liturgy helps us here. One of the church's eucharistic prayers asks that 'we and all thy whole church may obtain remission of our sins, and all other benefits of his passion'. The General Thanksgiving of the Book of Common Prayer, perhaps the most theological prayer of the sixteenth century, recognizes what these benefits amount to: nothing less than salvation, renewal, a life glowing with gratitude and promise: 'We bless thee for our creation, preservation, and all the blessings of this life; but above all, for thine inestimable love in the redemption of the world by our Lord Jesus Christ; for the means of grace and for the hope of glory.'

The cross is infinite 'benefit', literally, that which brings good to us. This and this alone is why the Gospels and the Christian tradition focus so heavily on the sufferings and death of Jesus. For St John, the emphasis is not on Jesus' pain in itself, rather on the good that comes from it symbolized in the blood and water that flow out of his pierced body. It is possible to read the Passion Narrative, gaze on Grünewald's crucifixion, sing *Stabat Mater*, watch *The Passion of the Christ* and, almost literally, miss the wood for the trees. We can respond merely as spectators. Or we can become involved with what we see – see it at depth as a sign of divine 'presence', as we saw in the first chapter. When Venantius Fortunatus in one of his great passion hymns celebrates the 'sweetest wood and sweetest iron', it is not to obsess about the instruments of a painful and ignominious death: it is to honour the cross for what St John says it is – the salvation of the world.

Perhaps no one has encapsulated it more effectively and movingly than George Herbert. We don't readily associate the understated, measured atmosphere of seventeenth-century Anglicanism with medieval or baroque excess. Yet one of his best poems, 'The Agonie', draws directly on the Passion Narrative and the long tradition of imaginative contemplation on the wounds of the crucified Jesus. The poem speaks of the two great mysteries of life, sin and love. Their meanings become clear at the cross.

Who would know sin, let him repair
Unto mount Olivet; there shall he see
A man so wrung with pains, that all his hair,
His skin, his garments bloody be.
Sin is that press and vice, which forceth pain
To hunt his cruel food through ev'ry vein.

Who knows not Love, let him assay
And taste that juice, which on the cross a pike
Did set again abroach, then let him say
If ever he did taste the like.
Love is that liquor sweet and most divine,
Which my God feels as blood; but I, as wine.

The poet, who knew his art better than most, does not baulk at a quite graphic description of Jesus' wrecked and battered body. Yet this marvellous poem, so Johannine in spirit, is shot through with the 'spirituality of gratitude' I am saying we need to foster. It is a beautiful expression of thankfulness and joy that the outcome of the cross, despite our complicity in it, is salvation and joy. The cup Jesus takes turns out in the end to be given back to us as the richest and best of drinks 'sweet and most divine' that satisfies, nourishes and heals.

A spirituality of gratitude is not only fundamental to Christianity but is the only basis for a balanced awareness of God and the world. If we take seriously St John's teaching about God's love, and how that love becomes ours not through effort but through gift (3.16), then thankfulness is the only possible response. This is the meaning of the Greek word *eucharistia* – and although St John does not give us Jesus' command to 'do this in remembrance of me', the definition of Christianity as living eucharistically would be entirely familiar to him. The most counter-cultural sign of this way of living, and its most attractive feature to those exploring faith, is (or would be) to live out the Gospel perspective of invitation and response, benefit and thankfulness, gift, gratitude and joy.

For St John, the source of this lies unequivocally in the cross and the Prince of Glory who is crucified there. A spirituality of the cross will abound in personal and social consequences. But what must drive it always is our profound gratitude that what took place at Golgotha was for us and for our eternal benefit. These are the 'goods' of the cross. Children sing on Good Friday:

> It is a thing most wonderful,
> almost too wonderful to be,
> that God's own Son should come from heaven,
> and die to save a child like me.

There is no improving on that.

*   *   *

Back in the garden, we now see how the sword brandished by Peter and the cup Jesus must drink are emblematic of the two ways that always confront us in the choices we make about how we live. Maybe it is a cliché to put it as the love of power versus the power of love. But as we try to live as God's friends and disciples, we know how tempting it is to fall back on patterns of behaviour that owe more to Peter than to Jesus. It is after all much easier to reach for the sword, whatever that may mean for us, than for the cup with all its dangers and uncertainties; easier to opt for power and possessiveness than for gratitude and generosity. If Peter had been motivated by *eucharistia*, how might his story have been different? But every time we imitate him, we are aware that at some level we are compromising the gospel with its clear call to renounce control over others and embrace the way of self-giving love. Perhaps what happened to Peter in the garden was as big a denial of his Lord as his threefold denial of him in the courtyard of the high priest's house.

In his memoir *The Railway Man*, Eric Lomax chronicles his experiences as a prisoner of war in the Far East during the Second

World War. Like so many, he was a victim of the Japanese obsession to construct the infamous railway link between Burma and Siam. He writes with brutal honesty about the unspeakable cruelty exacted by the Japanese on Allied prisoners. It is a real Passion Narrative. But the point of the book lies not in its record of hardship, degradation and pain but in what took place afterwards. Lomax found, not surprisingly, that his entire life was haunted by his POW experiences, and particularly by the memory of the Japanese interpreter whose collusion with his torturer became the focus of his pent-up bitterness, rage and longing for revenge (Lomax, 1996).

It took Lomax 50 years to realize that many of the problems he had faced in later life could be traced back to these unresolved feelings of hatred and vindictiveness. By a strange turn of events, he learned that since the war, the interpreter had become a committed Buddhist and had dedicated his life to promoting peacemaking and non-violence. In particular, he saw it as his vocation to remind the Japanese of their culpability during the war, and to foster expressions of both national and personal sorrow and penitence for the way in which Allied prisoners had been so harshly treated. At first, Lomax was sceptical of the genuineness of this conversion, but by stages came to see that a meeting between the two of them might be a defining moment for them both. So they met at a location that symbolized the tragedy, the Kwae Bridge. The pain of the Japanese man in facing his erstwhile victim was palpable. There developed an extraordinary sympathy and rapport between them that culminated in an act of forgiveness on Lomax's part: the first time for half a century that he was able to let go of his need to settle scores and, instead, find reconciliation and a new beginning.

It was a huge risk to take. Yet Lomax's story, and stories like it in which ordinary men and women put their swords back into their sheaths, not only inspire and move us: they tell us that the possibilities of love are without limit. They speak of how love is always a precarious enterprise, full of risk. Yet it is also infinitely strong compared with the sword; infinitely glorious compared with the weapons we imagine will make us secure. The cross is the ultimate invitation to discover a new way of being, what Paul's great hymn to love talks about as the 'more excellent way' (1 Corinthians 13).

Good Friday invites us to try out this path. Like Jesus, we are sometimes led along ways of struggle and pain: drinking the cup and walking the *Via Crucis* is normal human life for most people some of the time, and for some people all of the time. Yet to put away our swords of resentment – our instinct to kick back at life for dealing with us unfairly, to renounce the wish to hurt others in order to cover up our own hurt – all this is to open ourselves up to the redeeming, healing power of love that we see on the cross. The imitation of Christ is a direct outcome of the 'spirituality of gratitude'. Once we start living it, Christianity begins to look credible and inviting. Not to do this is to follow Peter down the route of denial – for without gratitude, there *is* no Christianity.

The Third Word

John 18.20–23

⇒•◦•⇐

'I have spoken openly to the world; I have always taught in
synagogues and in the temple, where all the Jews come
together. I have said nothing in secret. Why do you ask me?
Ask those who heard what I said to them; they know
what I said . . . If I have spoken wrongly, testify to the
wrong. But if I have spoken rightly, why do you strike me?'

The Third Word is about speech.

Language is one of the most precious gifts that we have. It is one
of the clearest identifying characteristics of a human being compared
to an animal or a machine. It is capable of infinite calibration,
nuancing and refinement, as the great writers and poets of
every culture testify. Even if it is not in itself an argument for the
existence of God, its existence is part of the evidence on which at
least one philosopher bases his case for not being an atheist
(Kenny, 2006, pp. 24ff.).

The Passion Narrative can be read as a story about words and
their power. It shows how words hold the possibility both to
destroy and to redeem. In this book I am, so to speak, underlining
the words spoken by Jesus in the Passion Narrative so that we can
hear them as sayings about our whole life. If instead we underlined
the words of other characters in this drama – the crowd, the soldiers,
the priests, Peter, Pontius Pilate – we would see the shadows
that lie hidden in human speech, the dark side that through words
inflicts damage and pain on others and fractures human society.

Take the second episode in the story. The scene has changed from the garden where Jesus has been arrested to the house of the high priest. The action oscillates between what is going on inside the house and what is happening outside. There is a particularly beautiful example of what is known as an *inclusio* here. The 'inside' event, the interrogation of Jesus (18.19–24), is wholly framed by events 'outside', where a parallel interrogation of Simon Peter is going on (18.15–18, 25–27). The text skilfully contrasts the outcomes of these two trials going on simultaneously. In Jesus' case it is, from the point of view of the protagonists conducting it, inconclusive. In Peter's case, we know the outcome from near the beginning.

Inside, Jesus gives an account of himself. Everything has been said openly; there has been nothing secretive or duplicitous. His 'Yes' has meant yes and his 'No' has meant no. As he will say to Pilate later, he has done nothing but borne witness to the truth. *Outside*, by contrast, Simon Peter is doing everything he can to wriggle out of the truth. In the courtyard, he warms himself with the servants. St John mentions this twice, as if the charcoal fire is a feeble, ineffective substitute for the fire of love that should be burning in Peter's heart. It doesn't take much for the first lie to be winkled out of him by a servant girl; then the second, then the third. In the first word of the passion, Jesus had twice affirmed 'I AM.' Now, in the darkness, Peter twice says the direct opposite: 'I am not.' The crowing of the cock is nature's own 'word' that draws attention to how a friend fails Jesus now that his hour has come. The bird's utterance is true to its own nature. Peter, however, has not only denied Jesus; he has been false to himself and his identity as a disciple. He drops out of the Passion Narrative at this point and we hear no more about him. It is a sad exit.

Annas, high priest *emeritus*, now faces Jesus. His interrogation focuses on his teaching. No doubt he wants to ask Jesus about what he has been saying. Has he subverted the faith of the Torah? Has he incited rebellion against the temple? Has he made blasphemous claims about himself? Has he allied himself with radicals and zealots who believe that direct action is the way to force God's hand, realize the apocalyptic dream, overthrow the tyranny of Rome and restore Israel to its former glory? If these are the matters that interest the high priest, Jesus' reply ignores them completely. It's as if he does not wish to become enmired in a theological debate with the clergy – always a dangerous tactic. It's only when he comes before Pontius Pilate, a man famously uninterested in the nature of truth, that he enters any sort of dialogue about his message and his mission. So Jesus deflects the high priest's line of questioning and instead defends the *way* in which he has taught. He has done nothing covertly, unlike this so-called trial that is taking place, probably illegally, at the dead of night. Everything is on the record. 'I have spoken openly to the world,' he affirms. 'I have always taught in synagogues and in the temple, where all the Jews come together. I have said nothing in secret. Why do you ask me? Ask those who heard what I said to them; they know what I said.'

This exchange is all about words and the way they are used. Jesus has spoken 'openly' – the Greek word is *parrēsia*. It means more than merely 'not hidden', 'not secretive'. It carries the sense of something said or done very publicly with confidence and conviction in its rightness: 'boldness' is how it is translated in other contexts. John reminds us that the living Word has spoken his truth in city streets and public squares, like the cry of wisdom in the places where people meet and do business (Proverbs 8.1ff.). Paul talks about how he has set about the proclamation of the gospel: 'we have renounced the shameful things that one hides; we refuse to practise cunning or to falsify God's word, but by the open statement of the truth we commend ourselves to the conscience of everyone in the sight of God' (2 Corinthians 4.2). And while the gospel is 'veiled' to many, this is because of the kind of message it is, and is not because of any underhand way in which it has been presented. The open proclamation of 'Jesus Christ as Lord, and ourselves as your slaves for Jesus' sake' is its own mark of quality assurance that guarantees integrity and good faith.

We need to pursue this. From the way Jesus answers, the presumption behind the high priest's question appears to be that this new teaching is something private and arcane, accessible only to a few initiates who have the key to this higher knowledge. Nothing could be further from the truth, says Jesus. His message has been openly taught because this belongs to its very nature. Far from concerning just the fortunes of the few, its scope is nothing less than the destiny of the entire world, the *cosmos*. 'The world' in its many manifestations looms large in St John as we shall see: society, politics, relationships, the human race in its totality. Often there is more than an undertone of hostility in the word: 'the world' often stands for those who reject Jesus' teaching or are indifferent to it (1.10). In this sense, what is taking place in the high priest's house is just another case of that pattern being acted out. But here Jesus' point is that whether they receive a welcome or not, his words belong in the public domain. 'The world' has been as much the sphere of his ministry as individual people have been. Whatever St Mark's understanding of the mission of Jesus may be, there is no 'messianic secret' in the Fourth Gospel.

*   *   *

There are insights here that can help the church think about the tasks of mission in our time. This Third Word of Jesus is about what we now call 'public faith'. Two themes stand out. The first of them is to do with the language in which we express ourselves as people of faith. How do we begin to speak about God publicly in a setting that is secularized, pluralist and multicultural? How does the Christian proclamation connect with people whose experience has become more and more insulated from the words, symbols, stories and rituals familiar to the majority of people in western Europe only two generations ago?

In a survey of recent religious trends in England, Hugh McLeod draws an apt analogy:

[These] religious changes ... might be likened to the situation in a country with many local languages, one of which has for long enjoyed the status of a lingua franca, but where the inhabitants of another powerful region resent this primacy and are refusing to use the common language: as a result, it is gradually slipping back to the status of a purely local language. This, however, has led to a very confused situation whenever natives of the various regions meet together ... In some areas of life Esperanto has been introduced. It offends nobody, but it does not move or excite anybody either, and it can only express a narrow range of emotions. In other areas, the atmosphere is more like that of an international conference in which everyone is allowed to use their own language, and participants attend a few sessions where the language is one they understand, and ignore the rest ... Large parts of the old lingua franca have dropped out of general use, but no more acceptable alternative has been found. In some areas of life the result is simply a void. In others, the lack of any convincing alternatives means that most people cling to the old words.   (McLeod, 1995, pp. 18–19)

One response to this religious Babel is to draw on the idea, developed by Walter Brueggemann, that 'preaching to exiles' will take the form he calls 'de-centred', based not on absolute metaphysical or historical statements but on the testimony of individuals and communities of faith (Brueggemann, 1997, pp. 38ff.). David Ford suggests that this means three things. First, we must 'articulate the full meaning of our own faith for others'. Then we must allow our testimony to interact with that of adherents of other faiths, aware of the risks we run when 'the deepest passions, the most zealous energies and the clearest illuminations' confront one another. But this is simply being honest about the 'ambivalent power of religion in our world'. And third, we must re-imagine the notion of 'boundary' between faith communities, seeing it not so much as a spatial dividing line as a point of interface and meeting that allows us to internalize the other's witness and let it inform our own (Ford, 1995, pp. 156–8). Precisely this kind of 'meeting' is practised in the exercise known as 'scriptural reasoning' where Jewish, Muslim and Christian scholars engage in an intensive collaborative study of their sacred texts and discover how enriching the conversation becomes, not just for the understanding of the 'other' faiths, but of their own too.

In all this, there is no weakening of the vocabulary, grammar and syntax of the language of faith. On the contrary, learning to speak of God in public in this way allows the language to be tested, purified and enriched. What will come out of it will be a way of speaking about God that as theology is more robust, not less, and that as testimony carries more conviction, not less. I do not in any way underestimate how demanding this is, not least in the degree of risk-taking and trust it involves. It involves leaving the comfort zone of the ecclesiastical drawing room where, so to speak, we sit at ease in our armchairs and converse genially with one another. This is what privatized religion comes down to. It also involves abandoning the crude 'hegemonic' rhetoric of mass evangelism so redolent of empire with its belief that by insisting loudly and for long enough on the 'old old story', the message will somehow get through. And it involves giving up the attitudes of suspicion, hostility and even fear that colour our dealings with secularism and with other faith traditions.

They may not all be conscious, and if they are, we may not admit to them. But our imagined props and securities are deeply ingrained. The loss of old certainties is always painful. The renegotiation of reality, and the learning of a new language in which to speak of it, are hard won. The church has not yet broken free of the lost privileged centuries of Christendom. To be de-centred is to take a lower place, and that calls for both humility and courage. But the gains more than outweigh the losses. 'Testimony to the truth' is how Jesus himself describes his purpose in coming into the world, as we shall see in the Fourth Word (18.37). Speaking of God out of our testimony as believers is to emulate Jesus himself in mission. As in so much else, the medium is part of the message. And we find that 'faith-sharing' generates confidence in speaking about Jesus Christ like nothing else. It brings about a recovery of a theological language that is authentic and comes from the heart as well as the mind. In an age when personal authenticity is everything, this is not only desirable but essential if we wish to earn a hearing.

And all this will help recover the sense that to speak of God is both a science and an art. The appeal of God-talk is not only to the mind: to restrict it to this is not only to rob it of its power but to betray a deeply flawed understanding of what a human being is. Testimony to Jesus Christ is as much to the affective side of our make-up – the heart, the emotions, the will – as it is to the cognitive. To speak of God at all is to enlarge the imagination, open new doors of perception. The words of our testimony are gestures that offer nudges and hints. And because religious language deals in heights and depths that ordinary language can never fully embrace, a great deal of what we say stretches language, pulls it around in ways that make it more like poetry than prose. It invites us to see in new ways, re-imagine our life within the bigger frame of God's love and truth. Of all the New Testament writers, St John is the master of this way of using language, so multi-layered and metaphorical, pregnant with symbols and images whose meaning bursts out in all directions. Alan Ecclestone calls St John's Gospel 'the poem we read' (Ecclestone, 1987, pp. 31ff.). That creates the right expectation of the book. As theology, it makes theologians out of us; as poetry, it makes us poets too. John's way of speaking sets a pattern for our own testimony. He is a safe guide.

But poets and theologians need to be humble before the language they use. It can only go so far. In poetry, and in religion, words commit us to both less and more than we want to say. We do our best with them, and with ourselves; but when we have finished, we know that Flaubert was right when he said in *Madame Bovary* that 'none of us can ever express the exact measure of our needs or thoughts or sorrows; and human speech is like a cracked kettle on which we tap crude rhythms for bears to dance to, while we long to make music that will melt the stars'. In the Babel of claims and counter-claims clamouring for attention in the market-place of religions, public faith may well turn out to be as much about what we don't say as what we do. There comes a point halfway through the Passion Narrative when Jesus' answer to Pilate is to say nothing. The poet of the Fourth Gospel is as alert to silence as he is to speech. So we must be too.

*   *   *

In the fifth century BC, Athens arrived at the pinnacle of its achievement. In his great funeral oration to commemorate citizens who had lost their lives in war, Pericles praises the virtues of a city celebrated as both civilized and humane. In a famous passage about public duty he says: 'an Athenian citizen does not neglect the state because he takes care of his own household; and even those of us who are engaged in business have a very fair idea of politics. We alone regard a man who takes no interest in public affairs, not as a harmless, but as a useless character' (Jowett, 1900, p. 129).

This brings me to a second reflection on how Jesus has spoken 'openly to the world'. In ancient Athens, democracy was not just about 'voting', but about active participation in the affairs of the *polis*. Like a useless Athenian citizen, a church that does not participate in public affairs is not merely harmless but is actually no good to itself or anyone else. The gospel is about the whole of life, not simply our faith as individual human beings. It concerns politics, education, social justice, economics, the family, the environment, science, art – in short, everything that concerns us.

Nowadays there is general acceptance even among politicians that the church has a legitimate concern for 'society', and that not to exercise this is to fall short of the gospel's vision. The church does this in many ways. Its proclamation of good news is of course primary. But it is also called to have other roles in the public domain, among them as celebrant, conscience, prophetic voice and source of wisdom to the nation.

It is easy to say that you change the world by changing people's hearts, but I doubt if it works quite like that. 'The world' is not simply a collection of individuals: it is a web of relationships, associations, communities and institutions. Some are small, some intermediate, some overpoweringly huge; most are 'real', but increasingly in an information age more and more are 'virtual'. Each has its own history, values, and the capacity for good or evil. Each commands our loyalties and allegiances in different ways, often without our realizing it, touching even very intimate aspects of our behaviour like the 'crowd' we looked at in an earlier chapter. Far from being autonomous self-determining individuals (is this what we would want for ourselves?), we are 'constructed' in a multitude of ways that are not all apparent to us.

Postmodernity can perhaps be understood as the first time in history when we have been able to grasp something of both the scale, diversity and complexity of 'the world'. This is both a problem and an opportunity for people of faith. The understandable wish to keep things simple can become a recipe for a faith that is over-personalized, nostalgic, secure in its certainties, not engaged with a reality that is too difficult and overwhelming to make sense of, let alone speak intelligently about. Fundamentalist religion (in many world faiths, not just Christianity) is like this. Its failure lies not in the passion and devotion with which its adherents practise their faith, but in its simplistic grasp of reality and its too limited vision of the power of religion to achieve the genuine transformation (rather than the coercion) of society.

The Fourth Gospel offers a very different way. It announces good news with the largest possible scope: 'God so loved the world.' Public faith means being true to this vision of the Gospel and not allowing it to be collapsed down and privatized. The church's mission always needs to live by a classic saying of one of the Fathers of the church, the fourth-century Bishop Gregory of

Nazianzus: 'What has not been assumed is not healed; but what is united to God is saved.' He was speaking about the incarnation: if the Son has not made the fullness of our human nature his own, our redemption must be incomplete. Exactly the same is true of the church's involvement with the world. God's participation is in everything: this is the world he has entered in Jesus. Incarnation commits us to a mission as global as that.

What this means in practice every church must discover for itself. Institutionally, the denominations can do much to galvanize a sense of common purpose as we try to respond to the large issues facing our society. The Church Urban Fund, for example, has successfully raised awareness of poverty and disadvantage in cities and urban areas. In the areas of peacemaking and inter-national relations, industry, racial justice and increasingly the environment, the churches have an honourable record of not walking away from challenges that are both big and intractable. Yet I suspect that it is not only, or even primarily, a matter of large-scale visions and agendas set by synods and church leaders. How we speak and act out the good news 'before the world' is much more for each local faith community to discern.

For example, Sheffield Cathedral is set squarely at the heart of the city centre. For years the cathedral community had been aware of the numbers of homeless and disadvantaged people who con-gregated in the area and came into the cathedral in search of help. This led to the setting up of a Breakfast Project in the cathedral hall to feed all comers with a cooked meal on a nearly daily basis. In a further development, an Archer Project drop-in facility was established in a nearby building at which people in need could find washing facilities, regular visits from health professionals, IT access, and educational, social and recreational activities. This activity is now being consolidated on the cathedral site as a result of a large fund-raising campaign. All this was and is undertaken out of an explicit belief that it is *required* by the cross. It is an attempt to live out what it means to speak 'openly before the world'. It is as central to the cathedral's mission as daily Choral

Evensong; indeed, because faith means loving God and one's neighbour, each is an expression of the other.

The German pastor and theologian Dietrich Bonhoeffer famously spoke about God letting himself be 'pushed out of the world on to the cross' (Bonhoeffer, 1970, p. 360). He wrote from Tegel prison in July 1944:

> The consequence for Christians in a 'world come of age' is that we must embrace . . . 'this-worldliness' – abandoning any attempt to make something of oneself . . . By this-worldliness I mean living unreservedly in life's duties, problems, successes and failures, experiences and perplexities. In so doing we throw ourselves completely into the arms of God, taking seriously, not our own sufferings, but those of God in the world . . . That is how one becomes a man and a Christian.
>
> (Bonhoeffer, 1970, pp. 369–70)

Bonhoeffer was one of the most courageous practitioners of 'public faith' in the twentieth century. He lived the paradox that it is precisely because the cross is a sign of the world's rejection of God that it becomes the inspiration for living in the world 'before God and with God'. His Christian challenge to Nazi ideology led to his execution in April 1945. 'Public faith' that is genuinely shaped by the cross will always entail giving up our lives, precisely as it did for Jesus. This is what it means to live 'before God'. We cannot speak 'openly before the world' until we have learned to live openly before God. This is how Jesus models mission for us.

*   *   *

Jesus' answer to the high priest is not only a practical programme for mission. It also holds an important theological insight about the significance of language and how words serve the gospel.

This third passion saying of Jesus takes us back to the Gospel's prologue: 'In the beginning was the Word . . . and the Word became flesh and lived among us.' This is the record of a God who has spoken from the beginning of time, indeed brought the *cosmos* into being through the act of speaking, and to whom nothing is more important than to communicate with his creation. In this, John follows the Hebrew Bible where the divinely spoken word is the means of God's decisive and dynamic activity in the world. 'By the word of the LORD the heavens were made, and all their host by the breath of his mouth' (Psalms 33.6). 'As the rain and the snow come down from heaven and do not return there until they have watered the earth . . . so shall my word be that goes out from my mouth; it shall not return to me empty, but it shall accomplish that which I purpose and succeed in the thing for which I sent it' (Isaiah 55.10–11).

By its very nature, the action of God through his word is performed openly. Its light is unassailable: it shines in a darkness that can never overcome it (1.4, 5). We are meant to recall this image as we read through the Gospel. For if Jesus truly is the Word of God, then every word of his bears witness to the truth and makes present the word of his Father. 'Anyone who hears my word and believes him who sent me has eternal life . . . Very truly, I tell you, the hour is coming, and is now here, when the dead will hear the voice of the Son of God and those who hear will live' (5.24, 25). In the next of the Eight Words, Jesus tells Pilate that everyone who is 'of the truth' listens to his voice.

Philosophers talk about speech acts. They mean the way language can be used to *do* things, achieve certain ends. The words 'I will' bring into being a marriage that did not exist before. 'I sentence you to ten years in prison', 'I agree to your terms', 'I forgive you' are all speech acts that show the power of words to bring new situations into being, sometimes irrevocably. In the 1950s the Oxford philosopher J. L. Austin gave a series of pioneering lectures called 'How to Do Things with Words' (Austin, 1962). I doubt that he had the Hebrew Bible or St John's Gospel in mind. Yet it turns out to be a deeply biblical concept. We could say that the creation of the world took place through a series of speech acts: 'God said: let there be light; and there was light.'

St John is saying that Jesus is the ultimate speech act, for in him, word and act are inseparable. It begins with the incarnation, Word made flesh. And throughout the Gospel, Jesus speaks to interpret what he does and acts to interpret what he says and who he is. The 'signs' Jesus performs in St John such as the turning of water into wine, the feeding of the crowd, the healing of the blind man and the raising of Lazarus, are given meaning through the teaching that is developed out of them. So we learn that we need the good wine of God's life and love to flourish; we are hungry in our deepest selves and need to be fed with the bread of life; we cannot see, and need to have our sight restored to us; we are dead in our deepest selves and must be brought to life through the death and resurrection of Jesus. In all this, words are made flesh and become tangible in the works of the man whom God has sent.

This reaches a climax in the Passion Narrative. For it is supremely at the cross that word and act become one. There we 'see', as nowhere else, the glory as of a Father's only Son, full of grace and truth. And like every other word of Jesus, this one is for all to behold. On the cross he speaks 'openly to the world'. His word is that God so loved the world that he gave his only begotten Son. His word is that he is 'lifted up' in full view of earth and heaven, so that all may have eternal life. His word is that God's purpose is to renew all things in his beloved Son.

*   *   *

Jesus before the high priest invokes a rich theology of words that takes us back and forth across the entire Gospel. His answer to the question about his disciples and his teaching goes straight to the heart of who he is and why he has come. But it falls on deaf ears. One of the officials assaults him: 'Is that how you answer the high priest?' Far from humiliating Jesus, the slap across the face merely highlights a well-known phenomenon: that officialdom in every age has only very limited resources of imagination. The professional gatekeepers of institutions, including religious ones, are often the last people to see what is taking place before their very eyes. As so often in the passion story, people who encounter Jesus condemn themselves by their words and actions: Peter, Caiaphas, Judas, Pilate, and this minor official whose name the narrative has not thought it worth recording.

It would be difficult to imagine a more dignified response to this cheap gesture than Jesus' reply: 'If I have spoken wrongly, testify to the wrong. But if I have spoken rightly, why do you strike me?' With that dignified speech, Jesus takes his leave of his own people. He has nothing more to say to the Jewish authorities. It has all been said already, as John has recorded in the controversies that occupy chapters 7 to 10. This night-time encounter is the final instance of what has already been foreshadowed in the Gospel's prologue: 'He came to what was his own, and his own people did not accept him' (1.11).

And that is its own indictment of a religion that has gone wrong. If organized religion has a role, it can only be to 'bear witness' in the public arena. It needs institutions to do this, and we should not be too quick to decry their importance. Whatever human beings decide to do together over any length of time will always end up as some kind of institution. It doesn't necessarily mean loss of vision, that 'first fine careless rapture' – though it can do. Institutions enable energies to be organized, memories to be conserved, experience and learning to be harnessed. But the Passion Narrative warns against investing too heavily in institutional religion. And when Jesus is presented, as he is in the narrative, as standing over against it and judging it, that must make us stop and think.

No doubt Annas and Caiaphas would have made credible claims for the faith of which they were the appointed public guardians. And it is much easier to judge with hindsight! But the warning is palpable. It could be inconvenient to us were Jesus to appear among us and start teaching and performing signs. If in our business as churches we detect even a hint of discomfort at the thought of Jesus speaking his Eight Words in our direction, it must be time to take stock.

The Fourth Word

John 18.34–37

⟫•⟪

'Do you ask this on your own, or did others tell you about me? . . . My kingdom is not from this world. If my kingdom were from this world, my followers would be fighting to keep me from being handed over to the Jews. But as it is, my kingdom is not from here . . . You say that I am a king. For this I was born, and for this I came into the world, to testify to the truth. Everyone who belongs to the truth listens to my voice.'

The Fourth Word is about kingship.

We have seen already how violence is a feature of John's Passion Narrative. Each of Jesus' first three Words is accompanied by an assault. In the garden, Jesus is accosted by a mob brandishing weapons. Then Peter instinctively draws his sword. In the high priest's house, an officer strikes Jesus across the cheek. These skirmishes have been between individual people – some named, some not. Yet the conflict is not really personal. From before the passion, it has had a political dimension through the increasing interest the Jewish authorities are taking in Jesus. By implication, Jesus is an irritant, to say no more, to the nation and its religious institutions. But now the power games begin to be played out on a much larger stage, involving nothing less than world empire itself, Rome, through its luckless representative in Judaea, Pontius Pilate.

St John's record of the encounter between Jesus and Pilate occupies a large proportion of the Passion Narrative. Of the story's

82 verses, no fewer than 29 deal with these scenes inside and outside the praetorium, more than one-third. In Mark's much longer account, Pilate features only in about one-eighth; in Luke, about one-fifth. Why this degree of interest on the part of the Fourth Gospel? Most scholars argue that, like Luke, John wanted to exonerate Pilate as far as possible from complicity in the crucifixion. For him, it was the Jewish authorities who bore most of the blame in delivering Jesus to the Romans to be sentenced to death. No doubt there was an apologetic value in demonstrating, towards the end of the first century at a time of persecution, that Rome had nothing to fear from Christianity, and that although they worshipped Jesus as king, Christians did not see their loyalty to him as a threat to their obligations as Roman subjects.

Yet this does not do justice to the significance John attaches to Pilate. Along with Jesus and the crowd, he is one of the three major players in the passion drama. As writers and artists have recognized, John's depiction of Christ before Pilate is one of the classic encounters of all time. It isn't simply that Pilate acts as a foil for the innocence and majesty of Jesus (though he does). It's that the praetorium is an archetypal place for St John. It represents what is universally true about the world in which Christians bear witness. In that place, two world orders collide: two kingdoms, two kinds of citizenship. Here corrupt human power comes face to face with the rule of God himself. It's nothing less than a clash of civilizations.

To anticipate, let me summarize what I think John is telling us about Pilate. He is the man who comes face to face with truth. But it proves too much for him, and he walks away from it. He may have made half-hearted attempts to protest Jesus' innocence, but his failure to release him only compounds his guilt. One commentator says:

> Certainly it would be possible in John for a character to proclaim Jesus' innocence without himself believing in it or caring about it . . . He is undeniably hostile to 'the Jews' but

that does not make him friendly to Jesus, for whose innocence he is not really concerned. Rather, his aim is to humiliate 'the Jews' and to ridicule their national hopes by means of Jesus' death . . . He is callous and relentless, indifferent to Jesus and to truth, and contemptuous of the hope of Israel that Jesus both fulfils and transcends.   (Rensberger, 1988, pp. 92–5)

The Pilate episodes are constructed with great skill. Like the previous scene darting in and out of the high priest's house, the Pilate scenes take place both inside and outside the praetorium. Outside, publicly, Pilate is the governor or prefect of Judaea, the representative of imperial Rome. His job is to uphold the honour of Rome, but realpolitik also demands trying to negotiate with the crowd, as far as he can, to keep the peace. Inside, the narrative takes us where the crowd cannot come. We glimpse Pilate the man and overhear a conversation that lays bare his character. We discover that whereas we had thought it was Jesus who is on trial, in fact the man on trial is not Jesus at all, but Pilate. This is Pilate's Passion Narrative too.

John has an intriguing aside near the beginning of the Gospel. He says that Jesus 'knew all people and needed no one to testify about anyone, for he himself knew what was in everyone' (2.24–25). In the praetorium, John draws the contrast between the man who 'knows' and the man who is ignorant, or perhaps we should say, between the man who knows with insight, and the one whose knowing is merely worldly wise and clever. The first reads human life with depth, taking in its subtlety and complexity. The other reads only the surface of the human text, never asking the deeper question, never probing to the heart of the matter. Even his opening question is not his own, as Jesus shrewdly observes: 'Did you ask this on your own, or did others tell you about me?' If it had come from the heart of a seeker-after-truth, the rest of the story might have been different.

*   *   *

The issue of Jesus' kingship is a crucial one (literally) in all the Gospels, but especially in the Fourth. When St John uses the word 'king' of Jesus, he does it aware of the risks he runs: of all the titles of Jesus, it's the one most susceptible to misunderstanding and misuse. At the outset, Nathanael the 'Israelite without guile' is the first to recognize Jesus as a man like no other: 'Rabbi, you are the Son of God! You are the King of Israel!' Jesus' response to this heart-warming outburst of faith is to encourage Nathanael not to make too much of it: 'Do you believe because I told you that I saw you under the fig tree? You will see greater things than these' (1.49–50). And it soon becomes clear that this slippery word sets up all kinds of misleading expectations. It only takes a sign like the feeding of the multitude for them to decide to 'take him by force to make him king' (6.15), at which point Jesus wisely makes his escape. Once again, we see the 'crowd' in action, true to itself.

Jesus' way of handling kingship language is reserved and understated. He deliberately distances himself from popular acclaim as if to say: you have your ideas about what kingship means; but I will show you a more excellent way. So he contrasts the shepherd-kings of Israel and Judah who abused and betrayed their trust, with the Good Shepherd who loves the sheep and lays down his life for them. The messianic ruler, entering his city on a donkey to palm branches and shouts of hosanna (12.13) turns out to be the Teacher and Lord who washes feet. And when Pilate says to him, 'So you are a king then?' he replies along the lines of, 'This is your word, not mine. But if this is the language you insist on using, I had better explain carefully what it does and doesn't mean.'

What Jesus says to Pilate offers the most comprehensive account of his kingship anywhere in the Gospels. 'My kingdom is not from this world,' he begins. *Basileia*, such a hallmark of Jesus' teaching in the other three Gospels, only occurs in one other place in St John. But it's a strikingly similar occurrence. There Jesus tells Nicodemus that only by being born 'from above' can anyone see or enter the kingdom of God (3.3, 5). The contrast is between being born of the 'flesh', by natural means, and being born 'from above', *anōthen*, that is, born of the Spirit as the mysterious gift of God. And this recalls John's prologue: those who have power to become children of God are born not 'of blood or of the will of the flesh or of the will of man' but of God himself.

Pilate does not know any of this, of course. But we readers need to carry the memory of these key phrases through the Passion Narrative as we read it. So it's clear to us that a complete contrast is being drawn between kingship as a human institution and the utterly different character of God's rule. It's not a matter of degree but of kind. There is an absolute gulf between the power Pilate represents and what Jesus stands for. Jesus' kingship comes from a source invisible to mortals. It can't be had except as the gift of God. And even when it's given, it can't be caught and institutionalized. It is stronger than any earthly power. But not everyone can see it. The test for Pilate is going to be, will he be one of them?

*   *   *

Jesus begins by identifying what it is *not,* contrasting it with the kind of rule Pilate knows about, the familiar Roman world of power politics and military might. Then he explains what it *is*, how his destiny as a king is not about coercive force but about 'truth'.

The evidence for what his kingship is not, says Jesus, is the facts of his arrest. 'If my kingdom were from this world, my followers would be fighting to keep me from being handed over to the Jews.' Of course, one of his followers did precisely that and brandished a sword, only to be rebuked for not grasping the true nature of the conflict. This is the same as saying that he had not grasped the true nature of discipleship. Perhaps it is striking that of Jesus' Eight Words in the St John Passion Narrative, two of them are concerned with this matter of how evil is resisted and the truth fought for.

A friend of mine recently took a holiday in a Middle Eastern country and told me about a museum he had visited there, devoted to the history and culture of Islam. He said it had been eye-opening to see how Islam was presented as a religion of the sword from its very beginning. Aggression, *jihad*, weapons of war were everywhere as the unquestioned assumption on which that faith was built from its earliest days. This seemed to be a world away from the teaching of Jesus of Nazareth. It is certainly hard to imagine the Prophet standing before Pilate speaking as Jesus does. He would never have condemned Peter for drawing his sword to defend him. To have followers who could have been fighting for him but were not doing so would have been taken as an admission of weakness, not of strength.

Many Christians find it strange and alienating to realize that other faith traditions have not only justified the violent defence of religious faith but commended it. Of course in our day, only the radicalized minority within Islam take the exhortations to holy warfare literally – with what destructive outcomes we know only too well. *Jihad* literally means 'struggle', but to most Muslims this image stands for the combat between good and evil fought in the hearts and minds of the faithful, an idea that is familiar enough from the Jewish and Christian traditions.

But we need to see ourselves as others see us. Large tracts of the Hebrew Bible read in Christian public worship tell of the wars between Israel and her enemies. There are commands to deal ruthlessly with the foe, shed blood without pity, even place them under sacred 'ban' which entailed destroying every last man, woman, child and living thing as a sign of their being 'devoted' to YHWH. Some of the prayers in the Psalms contain expressions of such violence that many people refuse to recite them in public worship. 'Happy shall they be who take your little ones and dash them against the rock!' (Psalms 137.9). 'I hate them with perfect hatred' (Psalms 139.22). Parts of the New Testament draw on the imagery of battle and bloodshed to describe the apocalyptic future and final judgement of the wicked. Sophisticated modern readers of the Bible have strategies for dealing with these 'problem' passages that don't include excising them from the canon. I am simply saying that at face value, the accusation of living by the sword can just as easily be made against strata within Judaism and Christianity as well.

I am writing this chapter in Vézelay in central France. In 1146, St Bernard of Clairvaux came here to drum up support for the second Crusade. His message was stark: the Christian lands in the Middle East were at risk of tumbling to Islam, and must be defended by force. That project was a disaster. Rivers of blood flowed across the Near East. An early outcome was that Jerusalem was soon overrun by Saladin. The site where Bernard preached is marked by a big wooden cross on the hillside. It's a beautiful and peaceful place. But to walk here is to be reminded of what it represents: bloodshed on a colossal scale, endemic mistrust – not to say hatred – between Christians and Muslims which continues to this day, the flawed vision of 'crusade' with its assumption that the cross, its shape already suggestive of a spear, could be turned into a physical weapon to be used against fellow human beings. In the backwash of this terrible history, the word 'crusade' ought never again to be used as an image of Christian mission. If Christians find the rhetoric of radicalized Islam frightening, perhaps our own Christian history has already helped to model it.

With hindsight, how prescient the words of Jesus seem! It's as if he has foreseen the corrupting effects of power on the Christian gospel, the distortions the use of force always introduces in the service of divine ends. To live by the sword is to die by it. For the root issue is not simply the destruction and waste of human life – that is the symptom. In an analysis of violence, the French writer Jacques Ellul identifies the disease itself. 'There is an unbreakable link between violence and hatred. Far too often intellectuals, especially, imagine that there is a sort of pure, bloodless violence . . . like that of Robespierre, who dispassionately ordered executions. We must understand that, on the contrary, hatred is the motivator of violence' (Ellul, 1970, p. 104).

Violence is a fact of life. Empires and nation-states could not exist without it, whether because of external threats such as invasion and war, or internal ones like the maintenance of security and public order. Political entities like nations have to be constructed defensively on the presumption (and experience) that humankind will not invariably live in love and peace. The soldier who wounds an enemy, the householder who stuns an intruder, the executioner who hangs a criminal does not (or should not) personally hate the 'victim' or feel the emotion of hatred. But whatever its legitimacy and justification, and whatever the love of nation or neighbour that sometimes requires it, violence is always bred out of a failure, somewhere, of love – especially when it is a purely personal reaction, as Peter's act in the garden.

And this is why Jesus emphatically rejects a kingship built on it, because his reign is based on an utterly different premise. It is seen not in territorial empire but the lives and relationships of those who become subjects of this kingdom 'not from here'. More than 40 years ago, Kenneth Cragg in an influential survey of Christian–Muslim relations pinpointed the redemptive purpose that marked Jesus' messianic call and for that reason ruled out any accommodation with political ambition:

> The pattern in the Gospels hinges on the meaning of the triumphal entry with its unmistakable repudiation of a this-worldly messiahship. Its climax is the cross . . . For his part, the prophet of Nazareth perfects the messianic loyalty chosen in the wilderness temptations and sustained through a patient devotion all the way from Galilee to Gethsemane . . . How different the finale might have been if Jesus, with all his strange authority over the populace, had elected to set himself squarely in the Maccabean tradition. Pilate would not then have washed his hands after a brief morning's embarrassment. The whole eastern empire had rather been set ablaze. But in no wise – that way – would the world have been redeemed. Jesus had no mind to overthrow the state, still less to displace it with another of his own, because he saw the salvation of the world in terms more ultimate than political.
>
> (Cragg, 1964, pp. 185–6)

Cecil Spring-Rice in his hymn 'I vow to thee my country' gets it exactly (and surprisingly) right in the second verse that any Johannine Christian can sing confidently:

And there's another country, I've heard of long ago,
Most dear to them that love her, most great to them that know;
We may not count her armies, we may not see her King;
Her fortress is a faithful heart, her pride is suffering;
And soul by soul and silently her shining bounds increase,
And her ways are ways of gentleness and all her paths are peace.

*   *   *

What does it mean, then, not to 'fight' but to live as citizens of this kingdom? This is what Jesus goes on to explain to Pilate. 'For this was I born, and for this I came into the world, to testify to the truth. Everyone who belongs to the truth listens to my voice.'

St John's language of 'truth' far transcends our ordinary ways of using that word. Philosophers hold different theories of truth. 'Correspondence' theories maintain that a 'true' statement is one that corresponds to the 'facts'; 'coherence' theories that a 'true' statement must be consistent with other statements known to be true. Both of these we feel intuitively to be right. But they are a long way from John's meaning. This isn't to say that 'truth' in one or other sense doesn't matter to John. He frequently calls himself a 'witness' and tells us that 'his testimony is true'. But it's precisely this language of testimony that takes us towards the heart of what truth is. John tells us that he is recording his testimony for one purpose: 'that you also may believe' (19.35). Belief in St John is never only belief 'that'. It is always belief 'in', entrusting ourselves to a personally committed relationship of faith that is no less, in John's language, than the knowledge of God and eternal life.

'Truth', like 'life', 'light' and 'love' is one of St John's big words. And, like them, it is really a predicate of Jesus rather than some independent quality: he is life, light and love; he is truth. In the upper room, in one of the great 'I am' sayings, Jesus has spoken of himself as 'the way, the truth and the life' (14.6). Truth is rooted in his own person, it is what he himself embodies. As the Word made flesh, he is the eternal wisdom of God made visible in an historical human being. In him we gaze upon 'grace and truth' (1.14) which is nothing less than the face of God himself. To know the truth and to be set free by it is Jesus' gift to his disciples. He prays for them before the passion, 'sanctify them in the truth: your word is truth' (17.17). After his departure, truth will continue to sustain them through 'the Spirit of truth' who will lead and guide them into all the truth (16.13).

In an important passage earlier in the Gospel, there is an extended debate about truth. It's part of the long dispute between Jesus and the Jewish leaders that we noticed in the first chapter, that culminates in the saying that so shocked the authorities that they tried to stone him: 'Before Abraham was, I am.' What leads up to this claim and their reaction to it is his accusation that

> you are from your father the devil . . . He was a murderer from the beginning and does not stand in the truth, because there is no truth in him. When he lies, he speaks according to his own nature, for he is a liar and the father of lies. But because I tell the truth, you do not believe me . . . Whoever is from God hears the words of God. The reason you do not hear them is that you are not from God.   (8.44–47)

Jesus draws an absolute contrast here. It is much more than the difference between 'telling' the truth and 'telling' a lie. He is pointing to the fundamental principles of truth and falsehood on which all life is ultimately based: 'the' truth and 'the' lie. It isn't easy to reduce such a fundamental concept to more basic terms: 'the' truth is the reality of God himself, and by extension, the knowledge of him as Jesus has revealed it. It's this truth-as-knowledge that sets us free (8.32) and enlightens us (3.21). To refuse it is to be in darkness where life and love don't reach. This is the place Judas occupies as the man who goes out into the night (13.30). It's the same in the praetorium. Jesus says to Pilate, 'Everyone who belongs to the truth listens to my voice.' That is a direct echo of what he has said earlier to the Jewish leaders. Pilate is no better than they, for he is no more willing than they are to listen to him.

Truth, in the way Jesus means it, scrutinizes how societies and individuals see themselves, often uncomfortably. It's a judgement upon each of us as persons, and all of us collectively. This undoubtedly has a political and social dimension. And while Jesus isn't principally concerned in the praetorium with matters of state, this is far from saying that truth is uninterested in these things. Truth has implications for all that belongs to 'human empire': the governance of nations, the leadership of society and the management of institutions. For example, we now require people who hold public office to sign up to certain standards. Among the 'Seven Principles of Public Life' commended as good practice for leadership, no fewer than five are about 'truth' in some form or other: integrity, objectivity, accountability, openness and honesty. (The other two are selflessness and leadership-as-example.) Study of them reveals how far they draw on Christian ethical thought, both personal and social. (It would be interesting to assess Pilate by these benchmarks.)

So there is an implication in this for the disciples. Jesus has come to testify to the truth, and so must they. This is why they must not be seduced by the exercise of power and fighting flesh-and-blood battles: their vocation is to imitate him. The character of the church is being defined here. For John, truth is as much an identifying mark of the church as love. We could say that the church is called to be 'aligned' to truth just as iron filings align themselves to a magnetic field. For the church not to be aligned to truth would be to forfeit its right to be identified with Jesus. And that would be to fall into the same state as those whom Jesus accuses of being 'of the devil'. This is a very tough judgement. But it isn't meant as a rhetorical statement. It's what John himself believes.

It would take a Bonhoeffer to explore what life together as a 'community of truth' would look like. Truth-telling, in the sense of open, honest, unafraid relationships, is part of being 'aligned' to truth, and this is the theme of a later Word of Jesus. But for John it goes deeper even than that. 'Truth-telling' is an outcome of loving the truth for its own sake, believing that truth is something to stake one's life on.

There is an analogy here with psychotherapy. The therapist's aim is to help people uncover the truth about themselves and live creatively with it. One practitioner writes about his work in language that has clear theological echoes. 'Good' therapy, he says, 'is at bottom a truth-seeking venture. My quarry . . . is illusion. I war against magic. I believe that though illusion often cheers and comforts, it ultimately and invariably weakens and constricts the spirit' (Yalom, 1991, p. 154). As a description of how the Johannine church needs to think about itself, it could not be bettered. The 'lie' in St John means precisely the illusions, fantasies, falsehoods and fools' paradises that obscure the light and keep us from even wanting it, let alone finding it. John is clear about the extent to which we are susceptible to the lie: 'People loved darkness rather than light' he says (3.19). The seventeenth-century poet Henry Vaughan put it like this in his poem 'The World':

> O fools (said I) thus to prefer dark night
>   Before true light,
> To live in grots, and caves, and hate the day
>   Because it shows the way,
> The way which from this dead and dark abode
>   Leads up to God,
> A way where you might tread the sun, and be
>   More bright than he.

If the church's mission is to have lasting impact, truth-seeking must always be at the core of its endeavour. This of course is easy to say and much harder to do – harder, that is, in seeing truth as going beyond making 'true' statements about orthodox faith or biblical morality. It's not disparaging theological and moral clarity to say that this cannot be all Jesus means by bearing 'witness to the truth'. Perhaps there is a suspicion among our contemporaries that the church's witness lacks 'passion', doesn't carry the conviction that comes from standing *contra mundum*. Truth-seeking is costly and difficult. *Martyria* is the Greek word for witness. It doesn't by itself mean death for the sake of religion or principle. But there is a dying to oneself involved in truth-seeking. Truth is hard won; to bear witness to it entails sacrifice. We don't need reminding that the Jesus who speaks of truth is on his way to the cross.

*　　　*　　　*

This is light years away from anything Pontius Pilate knows or cares about. Truth that is hard won doesn't register on Pilate's radar. His character has never been better summed up than in a brilliant sermon by the Victorian preacher Frederick W. Robertson.

Pilate had been a public man. He knew life: had mixed much with the world's business and the world's politics: had come across a multiplicity of opinions, and gained a smattering of them all. He knew how many philosophies and religions pretended to an exclusive possession of Truth: and how the pretensions of each were overthrown by the other. And his incredulity was but a specimen of the scepticism fashionable in his day. The polished scepticism of a polished, educated Roman, a sagacious man of the world, too much behind the scenes of public life to trust professions of goodness or disinterestedness, or to believe in enthusiasm and a sublime life. And his merciful language, and his desire to save Jesus, was precisely the liberalism current in our day as in his – an utter disbelief in the truths of a world unseen, but at the same time an easy, careless toleration, a half-benevolent, half-indolent unwillingness to molest poor dreamers who chose to believe in such superstitions.

This is the superficial liberalism which is contracted in public life. Public men contract a rapid way of discussing and dismissing the deepest questions: never going deep, satisfied with the brilliant flippancy which treats religious beliefs as phases of human delusion, seeing the hollowness of the characters around them, and believing that all is hollow; and yet not without their moments of superstition, as when Pilate was afraid of hearing of a Son of God, and connecting it doubtless with the heathen tales of gods who had walked this earth in visible flesh and blood which he had laughed at, and which he now for one moment suspected might be true: not without their moments of horrible insecurity, when the question 'What is Truth?' is not a brilliant sarcasm, but a sarcasm on themselves, on human life, on human nature, wrung out of the loneliest and darkest bewilderment that can agonize a human soul.　　　　　　　　　(Robertson, 1903, p. 297)

Ann Wroe says that he is 'the prototype of every uncertain man or woman forced into a dialogue with God. He asks, only half-believing that he will ever get an answer; what comes back is elliptical, disturbing; but for a moment the heart, like a door, has been laid open' (Wroe, 1999, p. 226). But now the atmosphere in the praetorium takes on an edgy, unstable aspect. The truth stands before him and over him, but he cannot see it. How he is unlike the long line of seekers-after-truth in John's Gospel, those who hear and respond to the invitation of Jesus' First Word, 'Whom are you looking for?' Some of them are nearer to finding it than others, but all are somewhere on the way to a recognition scene – Nicodemus, the woman at the well, the man born blind, and others.

Pilate could have joined this company. But he doesn't wait for his question to be answered. What if he had? Would he have changed his mind and chosen 'the road less travelled by'? That has to be our question, too, as we are confronted by the majesty of Jesus who is the embodiment of the truth at the heart of all life. If we are serious about our citizenship of this kingdom not from this world, then we must purify our vision of the truth. For the King who embodies it has only one throne where he summons us to accept his just and gentle rule. His regalia of a crown of thorns and purple robe show us where his throne can be found.

The cross is where this kingdom 'not from here' is finally revealed. There is, indeed, a collision of empires here. But it is more than the meeting of the power of force with the power of love. It is the judgement of truth on all falsehood and fantasy. 'Now is the judgement of this world; now the ruler of this world will be driven out.' And 'those who belong to the truth', who want to hear the voice of their King, know where to go and listen. They will find him on the hill of Golgotha, where his voice tells of God's work accomplished and of truth fully revealed in his broken, battered body.

The Silence

John 19.9

Jesus gave him no answer.

Eight times Jesus speaks in the St John Passion Narrative. But between the Fourth and Fifth Words there is a silence. Twice where Jesus might have spoken, he does not do so. This must be significant: what Jesus does *not* say is as important as what he *does*. Halfway through the book, his silence gives us the opportunity to pause and take stock. So this section is not a 'chapter' in its own right. It's more an interlude where words can be few.

We are still inside the praetorium where Pilate is interrogating Jesus. In the Fourth Word, Jesus spoke about testifying to the truth and listening to his voice. Pilate shows at once that he does not belong to that company. His riposte 'What is truth?' could not have asked a more profound question. But he doesn't have the seriousness of a real seeker. Without waiting for an answer, he goes outside to the crowd. Had Jesus bothered to reply, it would have been to an empty room. So he is silent for the first time.

Politicians, with power to wield and decisions to make, have little time for philosophizing. They have to be practical and realistic. To pause and reflect on the nature of truth seems like a luxury. And yet . . . if our leaders *don't* do this, how are our societies ever to become more aware and more responsible? Plato's vision of the philosopher-king has not often been realized, though a future Roman emperor would model it, Marcus Aurelius. Only one of Israel's kings ever prayed for wisdom. Pilate could have waited for Jesus to expand on truth. His tragedy is that he forced Jesus into silence on the very issue he came to bear witness to.

Pilate is 'more afraid than ever'. He goes back inside, and asks

Jesus another question: 'Where are you from?' But once more Jesus doesn't reply.

Why not? Isaiah says that the suffering servant was 'oppressed, and he was afflicted, yet he did not open his mouth' (Isaiah 53.7). Perhaps he has said all that needs to be said. He has already answered Pilate's question, for he has told him about his kingdom being 'not from here'. What makes this majestic silence stand out in the Passion Narrative is that it is *chosen*. It's a deliberate act of judgement on the man who is not of the truth, and will not hear the voice of truth. Pilate can win the approval of the crowd outside – for a time. But their noise only reinforces the silence inside where Pilate now knows that, whatever the outcome of this unwished-for encounter, he can only be the loser.

We chattering Christians talk a lot about silence in the liturgy. I am not denying its importance and have tried to cultivate it in cathedrals and churches where I have ministered. But it may not go much deeper than a wish for some relief from the torrent of words. Mystical theology would want to ask, what does God want here? What about *his* silences, *his* need for a break from our talkative liturgies? In the language of love, it's when the words run out that a profounder communication becomes possible. This is what silences in worship should be for – to allow space for meditation, contemplative prayer, the deepening of love.

But the silence in the praetorium is not like that. It feels charged as if a storm is about to break. In the book of Revelation, when the last of the seven seals is opened, there is 'silence in heaven for about half an hour' (Revelation 8.1). Then the judgement of the world begins, heralded by the blowing of trumpets. This connection between silence and the solemnity of judgement is portentous. The world is kept waiting, not knowing what will happen next, wondering whether to tremble. Silence intrigues us, keeps things mysterious and inexplicable.

St John is the Gospel of light and revealed truth. Yet for Pilate the time for disclosure is nearly over. Like the Christ depicted in last judgement sculptures over the doorways of medieval churches, his silent, penetrating gaze stares out without revealing whether or not there is pity or love within. Underneath, souls are weighed, like Pilate in the praetorium.

The Fifth Word

John 19.11

-->-o-<--

'You would have no power over me unless it had been given you from above; therefore the one who handed me over to you is guilty of a greater sin.'

The Fifth Word is about treachery.

In the Passion Narrative, different kinds of power collide: imperial, coërcive, brutal power, and the naked defenceless power of love. These forces act on Pilate like a vice. In the conversation between the man of Rome and the man of God, Pilate is more and more helpless, tossed this way and that like grain in a sieve, half wanting (to put a generous slant on it) to set free this prisoner who speaks about the truth, half needing to appease the crowd who are baying for blood.

The silence rattles Pilate. He returns to this favourite theme of power because it is what he knows about. 'Do you refuse to speak to me? Do you not know that I have power to release you, and power to crucify you?' It's the arrogant speech of a desperate man. Jesus' reply is the last thing he says before he reaches the cross. 'You would have no power over me unless it had been given you from above.' He could have chosen to ignore the question, as he had last time. But his answer to it is to continue the judgement of Pilate that his silence has already pronounced. He tells him that his imagined power is not his own. Indeed, Pilate is not 'over' Jesus at all. And whatever terror world empires instil in human hearts, their power is only for a time. One day, it will crumble into dust like the gods' Valhalla in Norse myths. Jesus' kingdom that is 'not from here' is different in every way. Its power has no end. So the power of Pilate to crucify and set free comes from the same source as the power of the man before him to lay down his own life and to take it up again (10.18). It comes from God.

This Fifth Word has been taken as giving divine legitimacy to the human political system that has Jesus in its grip. That is to read it in the light of other New Testament statements like 'Let every person be subject to the governing authorities; for there is no authority except from God, and those authorities that exist have been instituted by God. Therefore whoever resists authority resists what God has appointed' (Romans 13.1, 2). But this is not in St John's mind here. Jesus' point is neither to affirm the political system Pilate represents nor to subvert it. It's simply to acknowledge that it's a temporal, derivative power. Every Roman governor knew that the only power he held was like that. He was merely the local representative of the emperor, a servant of Rome. In particular, governors of Judaea were under no illusions about the significance of their patch. This remote, unloved outpost of empire was no Gaul or Spain, or even Britain. Perhaps Pilate expected Jesus to put him in his place by alluding to the obscurity of his title. 'You would have no power against me unless it had been given you by . . . Tiberias.' If so, it would have been a truism – an unkind one, but a truism nevertheless.

Instead, Jesus turns Pilate's riposte about power into a theological reflection on the divine origins of all human *exousia* or authority. That is to say, whoever we are, whatever we are, comes 'from above'. To recognize this is to learn how to handle power wisely and responsibly. Not to recognize this, to imagine that our power is autonomous, is to become corrupted and destroyed by it. This is Pilate's dilemma. No doubt, having crucified Jesus, he would have been glad to forget the whole episode. How many Roman governors were ever haunted by the memory of the people they had condemned to death? And yet, it's as if Jesus is promising that the memory of this day and these conversations will haunt Pilate for ever. Certainly he gained for himself what no other ruler in history has achieved: the unwelcome immortality of being mentioned thousands of times every day across the world where the ancient words are recited in the church's creeds: 'He suffered under Pontius Pilate.' Tradition says that, having been removed from office for incompetence, he committed suicide. It may or may not be true, but it's credible.

Christian faith commits us to name accurately where power belongs and to confront its abuse. As we saw in the Fourth Word, this means taking the side of truth against the lie. It calls us to stand with victims who are exploited and abused, because unlike Pilate, they have no power of any kind, whether their own or given to them from somewhere else. There are Pilates in every walk of life, men and women whose judgements are governed not by what is right but by what others will think of them, what the majority want, what their superiors tell them to do. They are creatures of the 'crowd' we looked at earlier. I have suggested that one way of reading the Passion Narrative is as a judgement on Pilate and what he stands for: the cowardice that breeds confusion and mistrust by walking out on truth. No wonder Pilate was 'more afraid than ever'. When fear dominates our motives to the extent that we are incapable of acting according to principle, we have lost our moral bearings.

I say 'we'. For we need to examine ourselves. It's a truism of Good Friday sermons that 'there is something of Pilate in all of us'. But it's true: anyone who undertakes public office knows that they put their integrity on the line, whether in politics, business or the church. All of us start out committed to upholding the standards we mentioned earlier: values like trustworthiness, accountability, integrity and selflessness. But if our high ideals are not to be an unrealistic fantasy, we need to know ourselves, and this includes our propensity for self-deception. We know how easily the vision we start out with can become dulled with time. Our choices begin to lose their moral edge and spiritual integrity. It isn't that all our good motives are discarded overnight, just that they are eroded bit by bit as the years go by. The little compromises that smooth the path of daily existence, the courage it takes to stand up for what we believe, our reluctance to take risks, our wish to please other people or be liked, our obsession with compliance – 'doing things right' at the expense of 'doing the right thing' – or simply the wearing-down effect of tiredness or boredom: all of this goes into making a Pontius Pilate. Like the sea that laps remorselessly away at the beach without drawing attention to itself, we scarcely notice the erosion that is happening – until the cliff collapses and brings the house down with it. This Fifth Word offers a reality-check. It traces the authority of every institution and every individual back to its proper source in God himself. To know where our 'power' comes from is both vital for our self-understanding and empowering for whatever our God-given task is. It's to realize that all work is both his and ours.

The church, then, has a particular responsibility in the way it orders its life, not only for what it models to the world but especially for what it should be in itself. In the Fourth Gospel, the church is not an institution constructed around power relations; rather it's a community of truth and love where leadership means washing the feet of other people and laying down your life. There is no quick fix, no easy path to servanthood. Our transformation from people fascinated by power into servants who wash feet doesn't happen by a kind of spiritual osmosis. The ceremony of foot-washing at the Maundy Thursday liturgy is one of the most moving rites of Holy Week, but it doesn't by itself turn us into people who are genuinely humble. That begins to happen only when we pay serious attention to the example of Jesus and make it our daily prayer to have the will and strength to imitate him. Only then do we acknowledge that to live as Jesus did can never be the result of human effort. It depends on *charisms*, grace-gifts that empower us 'from above', so that we can become what we are incapable of being by ourselves.

Humility is a spiritual task. It's to 'know our place' in the divine scheme of things, and understand that whoever and whatever we are comes from the *exousia* of God. St Benedict recognized this when he wrote his 'Rule for Monks'. Humility is the subject of one of the longest and greatest chapters of that remarkable work. It comes early on, for if a monk hasn't begun to 'know his place' in the monastery, how will he ever know it before God? The monastery is a 'school for disciples' – this is why Benedict wrote the Rule. It's tantamount to saying that it's a training ground in humility, for humility is learned through obedience. So the first of Benedict's twelve 'rungs' on the ladder of humility is to know that we are always under divine scrutiny; all our actions 'are everywhere seen by the eye of God's majesty' (chapter 7). One Benedictine monk writes about humility that

> it is the unwillingness to climb down and be like everyone else in subjection that constitutes pride, whether spiritual or human; so it is the willingness to stay small, and even look small, that gives its value to the performance of ordinary actions . . . Obedience is always humbling, but it is doubly so when offered together with everyone else and in connection with routine observances which afford no scope for ostentation and heroism. (Van Zeller, 1959, p. 100)

To find himself under this kind of divine scrutiny is precisely what is happening to Pilate. Everything that he has ever been has come under the gaze of Jesus. The Fifth Word cuts him down to size. 'You are what you are because of God.' What Jesus says to Pilate he says to all of us. Our human capability and potential, our 'power' is given 'from above'. That word, *anōthen*, reminds us once more of the conversation Jesus has had earlier with another man who knew about power, the Jewish leader Nicodemus. It's striking that the two words 'kingdom' and 'from above' occur side by side both in that conversation (3.1–8), and here in the Passion Narrative. Jesus tells Pilate that he must look upwards to understand the source of his power, just as he told Nicodemus that the only way he would see the kingdom of God was by being 'born from above', *anōthen*. 'Can you enter your mother's womb and be born a second time?' asks Nicodemus. The other Gospels say that we must indeed become like little children. What is Jesus telling Nicodemus and Pilate? That the journey of humility begins and ends in God. Without him, we shall never find it, and therefore never 'know our place' in the world.

* * *

Jesus does not stop there, though he might have done: what he has said about the nature and origin of the state's authority could have stood alone. But there is more to say about power and its abuse. 'Therefore the one who handed me over to you is guilty of a greater sin.' Who is Jesus referring to? And why *therefore*?

The first question is the easier to answer of the two. Pilate has already stated the facts himself, and used the very word Jesus now picks up: 'Your own nation and the chief priests have handed you over to me' (18.35). But the process of 'handing over' didn't begin with them. As in all the Gospels, John is in no doubt about where this 'handing over' originated. He uses the same word to refer to Judas Iscariot whose shadow falls across the narrative from early on (6.64, 71). We have known all along about the central part he will play in delivering Jesus to his destiny. Technically it was the high priest, not Judas, who delivered Jesus to Pilate (and some commentators take Jesus' Fifth Word to refer to the high priest). But Judas' role has been symbolically much more significant. So Jesus acknowledges that without Judas, he would not now be standing in the praetorium facing judgement.

It is not only Judas and the Jewish authorities who are engaged in 'handing over'. The word turns up again in the sentence which rounds off the long Pilate episode. His final act, John tells us, is to 'hand him over' to be crucified. In the deadly game of relay that culminates in the death of an innocent man, many different players are involved. John sees the judicial murder of Jesus as a collusion whose central act is one of 'handing over': Judas to the priests, the priests to Pilate, Pilate to the crowd. But we need to notice how the word reappears one last time at the cross itself. There Jesus bows his head in death and 'hands over' his spirit (19.30). Ultimately, what Judas, the priests, Pilate and the crowd do without knowing it is to 'hand over' the spirit of Jesus for the world's salvation. That is to reflect theologically on how human events unwittingly fulfil a divine purpose. Perhaps it recalls the words of Joseph to his brothers when they are reconciled: 'Even though you intended to do harm to me, God intended it for good, in order to preserve a numerous people, as he is doing today' (Genesis 50.20).

The word is *paradidōmi*. The root meaning is simply to 'hand on' or 'hand over'. It's how Paul describes the tradition that he has 'received' and 'handed on' to others (1 Corinthians 11.23; 15.3. *Paradosis*, what is handed on, becomes a technical term for the Christian tradition itself). He speaks about the Son of God who 'loved me and handed himself over for me' (Galatians 2.20). W. H. Vanstone has shown how the word is used as a marker in the Gospels. It indicates a transition in Jesus' career. Up to the passion, Jesus is the active agent in events: teaching, doing good, bearing witness to the kingdom of God. But once he is 'handed over', his role becomes passive. He renounces power. He becomes the one who is 'done to' by others, culminating in his suffering and death. The true significance of Judas' act, says Vanstone, is that he is the means through whom Jesus has become the victim, his destiny no longer lying within his own control but in the hands of others. (Vanstone, 1982).

This helps us to see the connection between what Jesus has just said about Pilate's 'power' over him and Judas' guilt in 'handing over' Jesus to Pilate. 'Power' as we have seen translates the Greek word *exousia*. Throughout St John, Jesus has exercised *exousia* – as the bringer of light, life and love, he acts with the authority and power of God himself. But now, instead of being in control of his own destiny, he is subject to the *exousia* of Pilate who can crucify or release him at will. That the Son of God by whom worlds were made should now have become the object of someone else's power marks a new phase in his abasement. And because of Judas' key role in instigating this, he is guilty of a 'greater sin'.

John is unsparing in his judgement on Judas, whom he calls the son of destruction (17.12). More than anyone else, he is the man who has used power for evil ends; or, we might say, been taken over and possessed by an evil power intent on destroying truth and goodness. 'The devil had already put it into the heart of Judas son of Simon Iscariot to betray him' says John (13.2). At the Last Supper, 'Satan entered into him . . . So after receiving the piece of bread, he immediately went out. And it was night.'

What does John find so unforgivable in the career of Judas that he uses the dramatic image of the night to symbolize his inner condition? It goes back to how he pictures the church as an upper room community. There, Jesus has much to say about friendship, and we shall return to this theme later. But I think we can say that the sin of Judas as John sees it is a sin against both the truth and the friendship of that room. There, Judas is portrayed as the direct antithesis of the disciple 'whom Jesus loved'. When Jesus predicts that one of them will betray him, it's the beloved disciple next to Jesus at table who asks him who it is. Jesus answers with an action of friendship, by giving Judas a piece of bread. The word 'companion' literally means someone with whom we break our bread: French children refer to their friends as *copains*. Yet Judas abuses the privileged position friendship gives. He throws the gesture of intimacy back into Jesus' face and leaves the table. The one abandons Jesus, the other stays with him all the way to the cross. Like Jesus himself, this disciple and friend loves 'to the end'.

In the ancient Near East, friendship was a sacred trust sealed by just such actions as were performed in the upper room: hospitality, foot washing, sitting at table, eating and drinking with one another. There is a sacramental dimension to these symbols of intimacy that are as old as humanity itself. So to break the bonds of intimacy and turn the power of love against your friend is to commit treachery. In the Psalms the laments of the persecuted sufferer have a lot to say about failed friendships. 'It is not enemies who taunt me – I could bear that; it is not adversaries who deal insolently with me. But it is you, my equal, my companion, my familiar friend, with whom I kept pleasant company; we walked in the house of God with the throng' (Psalms 55.12, 13). 'Even my bosom friend in whom I trusted, who ate of my bread, has lifted the heel against me' (Psalms 41.9).

We can speculate about what John thinks drove Judas to hand Jesus over. The other Gospels suggest the motives of envy or greed. These have undoubtedly poisoned many a friendship: *et tu Brute*? But the Fourth Gospel makes more of a rather different psychology in Judas. The first references to Jesus being 'handed over' occur immediately after the story of the feeding of the crowd, when Jesus foresees that people want to take him by force to make him king (6.15): here, at last, is the messiah who will rid Israel of Rome and give her back her freedom! This suggests that Judas is not the envious or greedy friend so much as the disappointed friend. As the Gospel unfolds, it becomes clearer that what he has hoped for in Jesus is not going to be realized. The delicate irony in John's use of the friendship-symbolism of bread points to these failed expectations. Jesus begins by multiplying loaves, and hopes of kingship are high. But they are progressively dashed as Jesus' meaning becomes clear, and by the time we reach the upper room, all he gives Judas is a single morsel of bread. The kingdom is not going to come; or as we know by now, it is not going to come in that form. Maybe Judas thought that Jesus' arrest would force the issue, but that is to speculate beyond what the Gospels tells us.

Like Pilate, Judas has intrigued the world for two millennia. One book about him has chapter headings that summarize some of the ways he has been viewed: as 'Judas the obscure: object of curiosity'; 'arch-sinner: object of horror'; 'villain: object of hatred and division'; 'tragic hero: object of admiration and sympathy'; and 'the penitent: object of hope and emulation' (Paffenroth, 2001). Whereas Pilate is someone we can begin to know, Judas is altogether more inscrutable. But for John, it is what he represents that matters more than what he is in himself. In the Gospel he is not simply the lonely, isolated erstwhile friend whose destiny is to become the most tragic individual in history. He stands for an entire community that has turned against Jesus and made him the object of their hatred.

John underlines this collective rejection of Jesus at the very outset of his book. 'He came to what was his own, and his own people did not accept him' (1.11). The theme of how his mission results first in misunderstanding and then in open hostility is present in all the Gospels, but in St John it features from the start. Subsequent episodes in the Gospel flesh out that initial statement about the man who was not welcome in his own community. In the bitter debate about his messiahship that we have already looked at, Jesus rounds on the religious leaders and accuses them of being from the devil (8.44). And when Jesus tells Pilate that the hander-over, the *traditor*, is guilty of a greater sin, we can't avoid the conclusion that St John sees an entire community implicated in his action. 'Judas' is not only the individual man. His name in Greek means 'the Jew'.

*　　　*　　　*

This is hard to say for someone like me who has Jewish blood in his veins. The anti-Semitism that has poisoned Christian attitudes to the Jewish community for centuries has found St John's Gospel a susceptible text as a source to feed its hatreds. There is no getting away from the disparaging references to 'the Jews' throughout the story that John tells. He portrays them as having lost all sense of spiritual direction. Instead of asking for the release of an innocent man, they clamour for a murderer and thug. Despite their hatred of the Romans, they appeal to Pilate to crucify Jesus on the disingenuous grounds of loyalty to the state. And worst of all is their response to Pilate's question, 'Shall I crucify your king?' They cry out in a terrible unison, 'We have no king but the emperor.' There is not a trace of hesitation or doubt in that cry. It's the ultimate surrender of their birthright, the betrayal of their identity as the people whose king is God alone.

This is how St John tells it. We can't gloss over how the Passion Narrative was exploited by Christians early on to blame Judaism for the death of Jesus. And the first thing to acknowledge is how late in the day official Christian recognition of these facts has come, together with the first serious attempts to address it as an issue in Jewish–Christian dialogue. I do not know what it feels like as a practising member of the Jewish community to hear the St John Passion Narrative read on Good Friday or the Reproaches sung. But we are learning as we read and handle texts to be careful about the historic resonances they carry for different communities, especially for those that have been or still are made victims in some way. Living as we do in the aftermath of Nazism and the extermination camps, we must all go back to familiar texts and ask whether, in the light of events, we have been responsible in how we have used and interpreted them.

My task is not to defend St John here: if need be, 'God can write straight on crooked lines' (Bieringer *et al.*, 2001, p. 34). But we need to ask whether his Passion Narrative hasn't been misconstrued and misused. The author of the Fourth Gospel was himself Jewish, as presumably were his intended readers, probably living not in the historic homeland but in other parts of the world in the Diaspora. And however far the church of his day had already separated from organized Judaism, it is hardly possible that John would not have felt strong affection and loyalty towards the community that had nurtured both him and his Lord. It's the Fourth Gospel that states categorically that 'salvation is from the Jews' (4.22). So it is not a question of some Gentile taking the moral high ground and berating 'the Jews' for their failure to recognize Jesus as Messiah and King. If John had not been Jewish, then some of his statements would indeed have been hard to forgive. As it is, he is acknowledging with sadness that sections of his own community had not been able to welcome Jesus. I see him say something like this: that with all that his own people have inherited in their scriptures, their history, their covenants and their native religious instinct, their refusal of Jesus is a tragedy.

Nor must we think of St John as projecting his disappointment or anger onto the Jewish community 'out there'. To recognize that he regards the people he is writing about as his own extended family is helpful. The Catholic theologian Donald Nicholl, comparing Dante to Dostoyevsky, suggests an analogy:

> It is a misreading of the *Divine Comedy*, and particularly of *Hell*, to think of the characters described there as external to Dante himself or as enemies whom he is judging in a pharisaical spirit. The *Divine Comedy* is actually an act of confession. Not, of course, that Dante was guilty of all the vices which are punished there: but all the vices castigated there are incarnated in historical personages through the power of the poet's imagination, and in the light of those personages the poet is able to see the hidden energies for vice within his own person. And by bringing them into the light he transforms them and is able to integrate them as healing forces in his own self. The same is true of Dostoyevsky. In all the characters that occur in [his] many writings . . . we see reflected the vices, temptations, betrayals, despair and unbelief of his age – by all of which he was touched as only an artist of great imaginative capacity can be. The fact that he was able to describe those forces of despair and nihilism so memorably is a sign of how profoundly he was touched by them.
>
> (Nicholl, 1997, pp. 121–2)

Could something like this be true of the New Testament's greatest artist? We don't know what took place in the psyche of St John when he became a disciple, and how large the issue of his own Jewish identity loomed then and subsequently. It's conjecturing to ask whether the Gospel's attitude to Judaism may reflect something of his own struggle, and whether Judas may be symbolizing it in the narrative. If Judas personifies the Jewish community, then it's not fanciful to think that he may personify a part of the evangelist too – as may Peter, Caiaphas and Pilate for that matter.

We can't help writing out of our own experience, shadow as well as light. But what we do know is that John's personal experience of Jesus was life changing and redemptive. He knew what it was to be greatly *loved*. He writes so that others may find the same life-changing friendship in Jesus – including his own people who he hopes and longs and prays will one day receive him.

There is one more aspect to this, and it's crucial to our reading of St John. While the actions of Judas represent the 'greater sin' of those who delivered the Son of God to Pilate, John does not mean to focus only on the flaws and failures of his own community. His global word for those who reject Jesus is 'the world', as we have seen. Jesus warns his disciples: 'If the world hates you, be aware that it hated me before it hated you' (15.18). In other words, Judas stands not only for his own people but for a *cosmos* of hostility and alienation, a place of darkness into which the light comes. 'He was in the world, and the world came into being through him; yet the world did not know him' (1.10). That is the predicament against which the specific case of 'the Jews' has to be understood: humanity's propensity to run away from the light because it exposes the truth of our condition. And, wonderfully, St John's vision is vast and generous enough to see even the world's enmity as something that can be overcome by the power of love. For it is precisely this same *cosmos* that God 'so loves', to the extent of giving his only Son (3.16).

All this means that as I read the Fourth Gospel, I see myself implicated in that 'greater sin' Jesus speaks about to Pilate. It is ultimately not 'they' who have handed Jesus over – Judas, Caiaphas, Pilate, the Jews – each of us has had a hand in it. This is not meant as another predictable piece of Good Friday piety. It is the tough truth about who and what we are, according to the Fourth Gospel. 'The world' in all its confusion, ambivalence and sin is reflected in microcosm in the lives and relationships of all of us. If we have the slightest awareness of ourselves, we recognize the shadow in our own souls, the part of us that goes out 'into the night' with all the betrayals that belong there. Our own complicity in the cross is absolutely basic to our coming to understand its meaning. For the question 'Who killed Jesus?' is at heart a theological and spiritual one. As Jürgen Moltmann puts it, 'For a Christian there can be no question of any guilt on the part of the Jews for the crucifixion of Jesus – for his history is a theological history; there can only be a question of the offer of God's law of grace' (Moltmann, 1974, p. 135).

In one of his great phrases, Dante calls sin *il gran rifiuto*, the great refusal. In the *Inferno*, hell is a funnel whose circles point ever downwards to its frozen heart where Satan is. Three others are with him in that hopeless, God-forsaken place: Brutus, Cassius and Judas Iscariot. These three have in common that they all acted treacherously towards those to whom they owed loyalty, and refused the grace and truth of friendship. This is where the abuse of trust logically leads. It's no defence to say that we have walked with Jesus, heard his teaching, seen his mighty works. The Sermon on the Mount warns against saying 'Lord, Lord' too easily. It's whether we say 'Yes' or 'No' to him that matters.

The Passion Narrative is not comfortable reading. It's a searchlight that probes our inner world, scrutinizes our motives, exposes our ambivalence. It can seem as though there is no mercy. But if we stay with John's story, we discover that it is about grace as well as truth. The judgement upon us is also our salvation: the light of truth that scrutinizes us also brings hope. We look into it and discover that it comes from an open door. Our great refusals don't have the last word after all. For that open door is nothing less than love's invitation and command to come back in again out of the night, and sit and eat.

The Sixth Word

John 19.26–27

‹——›◦‹——›

'Woman, here is your son . . . Here is your mother.'

The Sixth Word is about intimacy.

We have arrived at Golgotha. With the Sixth Word of Jesus to his mother and his friend, we enter the familiar territory of what we call the 'Seven Last Words from the Cross'. In one sense, it feels a world away from the five earlier Words. They have all been spoken from within the relentless movement of the narrative towards this point: in the garden, in the high priest's house, in the praetorium. Nevertheless each saying has provided a respite from the hectic activity, the bawling, the shouting and the noise going on all around Jesus, so that above the clamour we discern the larger truths that are at stake in the passion. They are truths about himself and his mission, about his kingdom, about the human condition, about ourselves. I have tried to suggest how we need to re-tune our reading of the Passion Narrative so that we hear these sayings in a new way, and uncover their universal significance.

The Seven Last Words have always been heard in that way. I argued in the Introduction that the tradition of preaching on all seven on Good Friday may not be the best way to help us understand the Passion Narrative, for they conflate the four accounts and that has the effect of obscuring the distinctive voice of each of them. But that is not to say that Christians have been wrong to see layers of meaning in them that far transcend the 'literal' sense of the words. Centuries of devotion have given them a numinous quality; and a 'hermeneutic of the numinous', something like what the medieval interpreters called the 'mystical' way of reading scripture, is as important as their literal or historical study.

Now, at the cross, the activity is almost over. There are still noises to be heard: the crowd complaining about the title Pilate has written over the cross; the soldiers rattling their dice. But these seem more distant. We have reached a point in the drama where everything is quietening down in preparation for death. The narrative focuses with great intensity on the cross and what is happening immediately around it. The last words of any dying human being are always invested with an aura of particular significance as the silence gathers around the scene of death. So in view of the extraordinarily artful way in which St John has constructed his Gospel from prologue to passion, and the array of meanings carried by his key words and images, we are now ready to hear in the three sayings from the cross symbolic utterances that constitute the dying Jesus' last will and testament to his world.

*   *   *

St John's account of the cross differs in important respects from the other three. For instance, John is emphatic that Jesus goes to Golgotha carrying his own cross (19.17), though the other Gospels say that Simon of Cyrene was pressed into carrying it. For John, this underlines how Jesus achieves the salvation of the world on his own, unaided. The early Christian Fathers saw this prefigured in the story of Isaac, who went with his father to the place of sacrifice and carried the wood for the burnt offering himself (Genesis 22.6). In that story, God provided a lamb for the burnt offering and Isaac was spared the knife that hovered over him. In this one, the knife falls without pity on the one who John has told us is 'the lamb of God'.

Then John makes much more than the other evangelists of the *titulus* or inscription placed above Jesus' cross. 'Jesus of Nazareth, the King of the Jews' it says, written in Latin, Greek and Aramaic, the three languages spoken in the Near East at that time. The title is symbolically important for John, for it's Pilate's last laugh on the Jewish crowd that has insisted that it has no king but the emperor. It's also his belated, if ironic, recognition of Jesus' kingship: 'So you *are* a king?' (18.37). But most significantly of all, it's the public declaration of who Jesus is: the King not only of the Jews but of all who are represented by the languages of the title; that is, the entire human family. It is an open statement of the truth 'before the world', in keeping with the way Jesus has always taught about himself (18.20). It stands for all time. 'What I have written, I have written.'

In John, the last three sayings from the cross also differ from the other Gospels. Their audiences are different. John does not have Jesus praying for those who crucified him, 'Father, forgive them; for they do not know what they are doing' (Luke 23.34). Neither does he have him turning to the dying thief to reassure him: 'Today you will be with me in Paradise' (Luke 23.43). Nor does he call directly on God from the cross. There is no cry of agony as in Matthew and Mark, nor a prayer of trust and self-offering as in Luke. Jesus in the Fourth Gospel takes his leave of the world in a strikingly different way.

But like Luke, John does depict a dying Jesus who *notices* those who are near him in his suffering. Echoing the (perhaps) four soldiers who are dividing up Jesus' clothing, there are (probably) four women and one man. The soldiers are indifferent to Jesus: they may well not bear him any ill-will personally but are simply doing their job. They have nothing to say to him now (unlike in St Mark, where they mock him), and he has nothing to say to them. But the other group are there because they love him: the Marys, the unnamed sister of the mother of Jesus, and the beloved disciple. John emphasizes that they are standing *near* the cross, just as the beloved disciple had leaned next to him in the upper room. They have not abandoned Jesus like so many others. They are his true followers and friends. They cannot help him in his suffering, but they can be *compassionate*. They can and do 'suffer with' him.

*   *   *

Something important is taking place in this little group of onlookers who are also 'sufferers with'. They, or at least two of them, are becoming a new community. The Sixth Word focuses on how relationships are reconfigured at the cross. 'When Jesus saw his mother and the disciple whom he loved standing beside her, he said to his mother, "Woman, here is your son." Then he said to the disciple, "Here is your mother." And from that hour the disciple took her into his own home.'

Why is Jesus so laconic, almost peremptory? Why doesn't he say, 'Mother, where I am going you cannot come. It's time to say farewell. But I want you to know that my love does not end here. Your welfare matters as much to me now as it always has. So I am asking my best friend John to look after you. Regard him as if he were your son. His home is your home'? For surely, at one level, this is an expression of Jesus' very specific care for the two people he loved best in the world. I say *two*, for I hear Jesus providing for the emotional welfare of the orphaned John just as much as for Mary herself. It's a beautiful act. It shows that 'suffering with', *com*passion, is reciprocal. It's happening in Jesus no less than in his friends. Even at the height of his own pain, he is aware of the pain *they* feel, and wants them to know that he is aware of it. And we are wrong if we hear in these words any hint of caution or reserve on Jesus' part.

What John is consciously creating at the cross is another of his great recognition scenes. We have come across these already in connection with the arrest in the garden ('Whom are you looking for?') and the encounter with Pilate ('Are you the King of the Jews?'). The Fourth Gospel can be read as a sequence of carefully delineated recognitions of Jesus, beginning with Peter, Andrew and Nathanael, and culminating in Mary Magdalen and Thomas. At the cross, we do not have a centurion recognizing the crucified Jesus with his 'Truly this man was God's Son!' (Mark 15.39). It isn't needed: Pilate has already provided it in his *titulus*. Instead, John gives us a new kind of recognition, one that takes place among his followers. He invites (as it were) Mary and John to face each other, and to see each other in the light of the cross. 'Here is your son: recognize him!' 'Here is your mother. Recognize her!'

What Jesus invites them to do is highly personal and specific. *Ide*, he says, 'Behold.' It's of a piece with so much else in the Gospel that is about the removal of blindness and the opening up of sight and of insight. The reconfiguring of relationships happening here seems to come out of seeing another human being in a new way. If, as I have been saying all along, the community of St John is based on truth and love, then personal relationships must themselves be based on the truth about one another that is disclosed when the truth about Jesus is revealed. In their way, they too 'bear witness to the truth' through open eyes that 'see' the truth that lies in another person.

In two of his books, Blake Morrison comes close to what I am trying to get at here. They are memoirs of his parents. Both were occasioned by their deaths, separated by a few years. The first moves skilfully between relating the experience of living through his father's final illness and dying, and recalling the man he knew in childhood and early adulthood (Morrison, 1994). This oscillation from present to past and back again portrays him in a way that is at turns funny, embarrassing, poignant and wise, but is always vivid, sometimes painfully so. The second uncovers the story of his parents' love affair and marriage as told through their letters discovered after his mother's death (Morrison, 2003). Here was a woman who had always been somewhat hidden from her family, and, it turns out, from herself too. In both books, Morrison makes an ordinary man and woman extraordinary.

No, I don't mean that. I mean that here are two of millions and millions of men and women, any of whom could have been immortalized in biography – and had that happened, we should know that they were all unique, and therefore all extraordinary. The research needed for the second book especially shows how 'recognition' doesn't just come. We may never glimpse much of the true life of another person, even if our relationship with them is, as we imagine, intimate. To 'see' the truth about anything, and certainly about another person in all his or her complexity and mystery, is hard won. These memoirs are simply acts of *recognition*. They demonstrate in literature what psychotherapists and priests are supposed to know already, that no one is 'ordinary'. Every person has a unique story, and it will always be endlessly fascinating.

Some people disparage 'confessional' literature like this, where we overhear something of the journey, search and struggle of others. Morrison's books might not have found a market much before the Aquarian-feminized 1990s. He tells us that while his mother didn't object to the *Father* book, she never said much about it once it was published, and didn't have her copy of it out on display. There is a difference between the generations here. But she could not accuse either book of sentimentality and the distortions it brings to human relationships. The books are tough on his parents, though not as tough as they are on the author himself – and this is the person we learn most about. Self-knowledge and seeing into the life of another human being walk hand in hand.

*　　　*　　　*

How do we learn to recognize the truth about other people, and honour it in our dealings with them? This is a big question in an age when fantasy and feeling govern so much in our personal relationships. This scene at the foot of the cross, where recognition in the truth defines how love is expressed, has much to tell us.

One of the ways of reading John's Gospel is to see the coming of Jesus into the world as restoring to it a lost intimacy. 'Darkness' throughout the Gospel stands for the fracture and disconnection that the world experiences at every level. It stems from the estrangement from God described in the prologue as not 'knowing' or 'accepting' him (1.10, 11). And this spiritual disorder that infects the fundamental layer of human life is expressed as disorders infecting every other level. Estrangement from God leads to estrangement from our fellow human beings and from the created order. Like a pane of glass, damage to one part leads to the shattering of all of it. Disconnection and flaw run through the entire life of the human race.

When Jesus comes, it is as the light that enables human beings to see once again, and this means not simply observing but recognizing. Those who recognize Jesus come to believe in him. This is fleshed out by an array of other words and phrases that give the Fourth Gospel its unmistakable character: to 'know', to 'abide in' and supremely, to 'love'. 'Love' has at least four profound aspects in St John. There is the love the Father has for the Son. This is shown in turn in the love Jesus has for his disciples: 'As the Father has loved me, so I have loved you' (15.9). To respond to this love is to do two things: give love back to Jesus: 'If you love me, you will keep my commandments' (14.15); and replicate it in all our human relationships: 'Just as I have loved you, you also should love one another' (13.34).

In an age when 'love' can mean everything and nothing, it's important to be clear what John doesn't mean. For us, 'love' tends more than anything else to be a feeling or an affect. We fall into it, and (as divorcing couples say nowadays) out of it. It happens *to* us: we are its helpless (and hapless) victims. In his influential study of the origins and influence of the idea of 'romantic love', Denis de Rougemont takes the story of Tristan and Iseult as the paradigm of how love 'happens' to people. It's a morality tale whose theme is how romantic love trumps duty and loyalty. As lovers of Wagner's *Tristan und Isolde* know, Tristan is bringing Iseult back from Ireland to his native land of Cornwall as a bride for his uncle and king. But at sea, they both drink a fatal love potion. The spell is cast, and there is no rescuing the intoxicated lovers. But this is of course an act of treason against the king: in the end, their love destroys them both. But what is this 'love' they have for each other? With brilliant insight, de Rougemont concludes:

Tristan and Iseult do not love one another . . . What they love is love and being in love. They behave as if aware that whatever obstructs love must endure and consolidate it in the heart of each and intensify it infinitely in the moment they reach the absolute obstacle, which is death. Tristan loves the awareness that he is loving far more than he loves Iseult the Fair. And Iseult does nothing to hold Tristan. All she needs is her passionate dream. Their need of one another is in order to be aflame.   (de Rougemont, 1960, p. 41)

This is now the universal currency of 'love' and there can be few people in the West who have not felt its power. This isn't to say that *eros*, love as desire, isn't an important component of *agapē*, St John's word for God's love for the world. Spiritual guides down the ages have laid great stress on how desire for God is the first step in the movement of love towards union with him. We shall come back to this point in the Seventh Word.

But, for John, love originates in a quite different place. It looks, not at the experience itself, but at the other person. Its exemplar is God himself who 'so loved' (3.16). Love is the choice God has made to be intimate with his world once again. One of the words the Fourth Gospel uses to describe this is friendship. What distinguishes friendship from other loves is that it has no other aim than itself. It is not there to provide economic security or bring up children or defend the nation. It is not chosen for us by others: we enter it freely. It is altruistic, for our friend's welfare matters to us as much as – perhaps more than – our own. So friendship gives John the category he needs to speak about the love that is the model for all other loving. 'No one has greater love than this, to lay down one's life for one's friends' (15.13). 'I do not call you servants any longer, because the servant does not know what the master is doing; but I have called you friends, because I have made known to you everything that I have heard from my Father' (15.15).

When Jesus tells his disciples to love one another, he is commanding them to enter into the intimacy of true friendship. This comes down to saying that for John, love-as-friendship, this chosen, altruistic *agapē* is the primary category of all loving relationships. So at the cross we see Jesus urging his mother and the beloved disciple to befriend each other. When he commits them to each other's care, 'Here is your son ... Here is your mother', it isn't to engender unhealthy dependencies. It's to invite two adult human beings to see each other in the truth brought about by Jesus on the cross, and in the light of that recognition to act as friends to each other, take on the commitments of an intimacy in which the good of the other is the paramount concern.

This brings us back to John's vision for the church as a community of truth and love – or as we can now put it, truth and friendship. What is taking place around the cross is precisely what he has been speaking about in the upper room. A new community is being born here. It's the creation of the cross itself, because Jesus' way of loving at the cross brings new intimacies into being. And how this 'church' is to live will be modelled on the cross: servanthood, humility, truth, love laid down. In a recent book about how Christian theology reflects on the issues of power, Stephen Sykes speaks of the death of Christ as 'community creating'. He reminds us how the early Christian communities,

> as they reproduced themselves in the ancient world in a variety of new contexts saw the closest connection between Jesus' death and the attitudes needed to sustain these communities. They taught the absolute necessity of humility. There were to be no 'rabbis', 'fathers' or 'teachers' ... Rivalry and personal vanity were to be given up. Christ's humility in accepting death by crucifixion was to inform their bearing towards one another. (Sykes, 2006, p. 131)

It's a long way from the church we know much of the time. And even when we think we have touched the reality for an instant, it's only ever a partial glimpse that vanishes from our eyes like a chimera. We know that John was not naïve about this. His letters with their radiant vision of the primacy of love also show how compromised that vision had become in his own time. The conflicted atmosphere of much of the Fourth Gospel is the background against which the upper room shines out as the impossible dream that nevertheless remains the goal of every Christian community in every age.

It's easy to be caught up in glowing rhetoric. How does it become real in practice? At a time when the worldwide Anglican communion is at risk of breaking up, and when friendship and truth are at a premium globally, we can at least begin where we are, with the local and the particular, in the hope that our own expression of 'church' might show some of the signs of the community created at the cross.

One example of it is the experiment in church life tried out at Darnall, an urban parish in the east end of Sheffield in the 1940s, 1950s and 1960s. The incumbent for nearly three decades was Alan Ecclestone, a gifted theologian who had dedicated his life to ministry in 'tough' parishes. He had drunk deep at the well of the Fourth Gospel, as one of his books shows (Ecclestone, 1987). He believed that John's understanding of a non-hieratic church of truth and friendship needed to be taken seriously. So early on he began the famous 'parish meeting', a weekly gathering whose aim was to realize the true nature of the local church as a community of people committed to living the way of Christ. Some of the agenda concerned purely parochial issues. Much of it showed a passionate concern for 'public faith': debates ranged across nuclear power, gender and sexuality, the bomb, general elections and international issues of the day. But what its members recalled most vividly was how face-to-face meeting brought them into a wholly new awareness of truth and friendship:

Christian living . . . means that henceforth we are not isolated people, living to ourselves and answerable only to ourselves, but that we are members of one Body, living out our lives in and through this Body, and always both answerable to it and dependent on it . . . The meeting of those who are learning to love one another . . . is the channel of the deepest experience of beauty and goodness that we can know, but it is a costly business to give oneself to it. No wonder then that we are tempted and persuaded to fall back upon less demanding relationships, to accept substitutes, to make do with what professes to be a true communion of persons but is not. (Gorringe, 1994, pp. 102–3)

It sounds simple. Yet its consequences were profound. Parishioners spoke about finding their voice, learning how to love, being empowered for discipleship in a way that was certainly unusual, if not unique. This risky undertaking involved the renunciation of priestly power, which is perhaps why it has not often been imitated. But this humane, Johannine way of 'being church' shows what can be done when Christians take the words of Jesus and set about being a community formed by the cross where Jesus bequeathes us to one another's care.

*   *   *

We must turn finally to Mary herself. We have only met her once before in the Gospel. That was at the wedding at Cana in Galilee where she intervened to help the bridal couple whose wine – and happiness – was about to run out. John says that by turning water into wine, Jesus performed the first of his signs and 'revealed his glory; and his disciples believed in him' (2.11). Cana is meant to be emblematic of how the other 'signs' in his book are to be read. The signs disclose glory, and glory leads to faith – this is John's theology. His whole Gospel is encased by the two ideas. At the beginning, we see the glory of the incarnate Word, full of grace and truth (1.14). At the end, John tells us that all along, his purpose has been to bring us to faith in the Messiah and find life.

If Cana is the first sign, Golgotha is the last. There are strong links between the two stories. At Cana his mother intervenes to ask Jesus to do something about the wine. He replies enigmatically that his 'hour' has not yet come. But as we read on we learn what this 'hour' will be: the time of Jesus' suffering and death. On the threshold of his passion, Jesus prays: 'What should I say – "Father, save me from this hour"? No, it is for this reason that I have come to this hour. Father, glorify your name' (12.27–8). 'Hour' and 'glory' belong together at the cross. So at Cana, when Jesus speaks of his 'hour' and the story is rounded off by a reference to his 'glory', we know that the passion is in view. And the wine of Cana is echoed when Jesus speaks of himself as the true vine (15.1), and when John tells of the blood and water pouring out of the pierced side of the crucified Lord (19.34, 35).

Then there is the presence of Mary. 'Woman', he calls her on both occasions – to our surprise and even shock: in the ancient world, no son would ever address his mother in that way. But this is the point. To call her 'woman', far from being discourteous or perfunctory, is to acknowledge her symbolic importance in both stories. At Cana, she is present when the pouring out of wine leads to the happiness of many people. At the cross, she is present when the pouring out of blood leads to the happiness of the whole world. When Jesus addresses her as 'woman', he is recalling the archetypal woman of the creation story, Eve, 'the mother of all living' (Genesis 3.20). Jesus' words at the cross, 'Woman, here is your son . . . Here is your mother', are echoes of not only the wedding at Cana, but the more ancient story of the birth of the human race.

So there is a mystical symbolism in the presence of Mary 'the woman' at the cross. She becomes the mother of the disciple who saw, bore witness, believed and, above all, knew he was loved. He stands for all who follow Jesus in every age and in every place. And Mary the new Eve becomes in a spiritual sense the mother of all who believe and, through their faith, all who live. He takes her to 'his own' – not simply his physical home and care, but into a relationship of love that is as intimate and precious as the friendship he has known from Jesus.

What Jesus brings into being at the cross is nothing less than a new holy family. I believe that John wants us to appreciate how the intimacy inaugurated here moves beyond the limitations of time and space, for believers are brought into relationship not only with one another but with all who have stood at the foot of the cross in every age. We are drawn into a *koinonia* at Golgotha, a communion of saints symbolized by Mary and John. They have become our companions, fellow-travellers and friends. In particular, Mary the mother of Jesus becomes our mother. In heart and imagination, we stand alongside her at the cross and sing *Stabat Mater*, for we share her pain at the suffering of her Son. But we also rejoice with her at the completion of her Son's work and the salvation he brings to the world. The prayer known as the *Ave Maria* concludes: 'Holy Mary, Mother of God, pray for us sinners now and in the hour of our death.' That petition invokes our closeness with her at the cross as members of this holy family. And it recalls how she first stood by her own Son, shared his pain and prayed for him in his approaching death. What she did for him, she does for us. It's one of the most precious gifts of Golgotha.

In the cathedral at Lübeck in northern Germany there is a magnificent rood screen. It was created in the late fifteenth century by one of the most famous sculptors of his day, Bernt Notke. Its sculpture is of the highest quality. Like every medieval rood, it has a great crucifix as its centrepiece. At the ends of the rood loft are the figures of Adam and Eve, quite small. The figures nearer the cross are much larger, as if closeness to the crucified Jesus enlarges and expands us into our full potential as men and women. On one side is Mary the mother of Jesus, on the other John the beloved disciple. But nearest of all are two more figures. Mary Magdalen is kneeling on the left. On the right, where we might expect to see one of the other Marys, the sculptor has introduced someone else entirely, kneeling before the crucifix. He is a bishop in cope and mitre holding his staff, in fact Albert Krummedick who commissioned the work of art for his cathedral.

At first sight it seems a conceit that a bishop in his regalia should position himself in a place of honour alongside saints and in full view of worshippers. But his inclusion is saying the exact opposite. He is reminding us that this is precisely where we belong – with the saints, kneeling at the foot of the cross in this new community of friendship and truth that Jesus' death creates, bringing nothing to offer of our own except to acknowledge with gratitude the source of our life and our salvation. This is borne out by the bishop's gentle face, exquisitely carved so as to communicate rapt contemplation and quiet joy.

It is moving to think of ourselves as belonging in this noble company. Yet this is how we are meant to read the Passion Narrative. John asks us, 'Were you there when they crucified my Lord?' To answer 'Yes' to that question is to know that we are as beloved to Jesus as the disciple was. It is true that we look with sorrow on the one we ourselves have pierced (19.37). But it is also true that we look with joy on the one who calls us friends. For at Golgotha, Jesus says to us, 'Behold!' And our eyes are opened to the love that searches us out and knows us.

The Seventh Word

John 19.29

———⊷•⊶———

'I am thirsty.'

The Seventh Word is about desire.

When I was a teenager singing the treble line in Bach's *St John Passion*, I used to wonder why the three last words from the cross in St John did not have the tragic drama and pathos of the other three Gospels. Compared to the agonized cry from the cross in Matthew and Mark, 'My God, my God, why have you forsaken me?', St John's 'It is finished' merely seemed to state the obvious: colourless and matter-of-fact. While Luke shows Jesus unforgettably praying for the forgiveness of his enemies and comforting the dying thief, John simply has him making domestic arrangements for his mother: homely, but not portentous. While the others concentrate on the awful darkness and suffering of Jesus, John records him asking for a drink in words which, read out loud on Good Friday, can easily sound like bathos.

Of course as we learn to read the Fourth Gospel we realize that nothing is what it seems. The text is like a kaleidoscope: you turn it this way and that, and the light plays on its shapes and colours in an infinite variety of ways. Throughout the story, words we at first took at face value expand with new and unexpected meanings: 'glory', 'hour', 'king', 'truth', 'life', 'see', 'cup'. The face value is still there, of course, but immeasurably filled out and enriched by resonances from the Gospel itself, from the scriptures, and from the culture of the ancient world. We have already seen the layers of significance enfolded in Jesus' Sixth Word to his mother and his friend. The same is true in abundance of the last two Words from the cross as well.

But we must stay with the face value to begin with. 'I am thirsty.' Perhaps we don't expect St John, of all people, theologian of the Word made flesh, to notice the human experience of Jesus very much. And yet his Gospel is full of it: his hunger and thirst, his need for friendship and his enjoyment of company, his feeling for victims, his tears at the death of someone he loved, his horror at his own impending death. This is a writer who takes 'flesh' with the utmost seriousness, for the incarnation, the 'en-fleshment' of God's Son, is the very cornerstone of his Gospel. Indeed, he is explicit about this in his first letter where the church appears to be divided over this very issue. The touchstone of truth is to confess that 'Jesus Christ has come in the flesh', he says (1 John 4.2–3). The ordinariness of Jesus and his human needs are vital evidence about the flesh-and-blood human being he really is.

More than that, John's focus on ordinary things at the climax of the Passion Narrative is very true to the experience of dying. The literature of suffering and death suggests that whereas many people hope that on their deathbeds they will be overtaken by sublime thoughts (and be remembered for having uttered universal truths before dropping off this mortal coil), the reality is that the mundane and the commonplace assume enormous importance in the final stages of life. Anyone who has sat at the bedside of someone who is dying knows that thirst is one of the last cravings of the body to persist after other needs have shut down. Blake Morrison, whose books about his parents I referred to in the previous chapter, chronicles the day-to-day decline of his father as he nears death. It's not the spirit but the failing body that is at the forefront of everyone's attention – this once strong, manly frame that is now exposed in all its awkward, recalcitrant, even repellent ordinariness. John's Seventh Word, 'I thirst', is apt this close to death:

Upright now, he's mumbly, breathless, and wants a drink . . .
I put a towel under his chin, and tip his head back, and he
forces a bit down, and lot more comes back up, his hands

shaking as he tries to steady them round the glass. 'Is that better?' I ask, and he manages 'Yes', and then I try him with a straw, aiming its end between his teeth, and he gets the idea, seems too weak at first to draw anything up, but then makes a stupendous effort, the indents under each ear drawn in fiercely as he sucks, sucks. A drop of water makes it into him, and as he struggles for breath again I imagine, no *hear*, this drop of water he's swallowed pinballing down and through and into the dry places inside.   (Morrison, 1993, pp. 144–5)

*   *   *

'I am thirsty': in Greek, *dipsō*, the shortest and tersest of all the Eight Words. But it is the only one to be introduced by one of John's favourite formulae, 'in order to fulfil the scripture'. 'A jar full of sour wine was standing there. So they put a sponge full of the wine on a branch of hyssop and held it to his mouth.' Jesus' thirst and the offering of sour wine fulfils, says St John, a saying in one of the psalms of suffering: 'for my thirst they gave me vinegar to drink' (Psalms 69.21). This psalm, like Psalm 22 which St John has quoted earlier in connection with the soldiers casting lots for Jesus' robe, is one of those texts the New Testament writers most often turn to as they reflect on how Jesus died 'according to the scriptures'.

There are many important aspects to this quotation. John is referring back to one of the laments of the Psalter. We think of the Psalter as a book of praise (that is the literal meaning of the word 'psalm' in Hebrew). So it comes as a surprise to find that there are more laments among the psalms than anything else, and of those, most are laments of an individual sufferer. The kind of suffering that gives rise to these laments varies from psalm to psalm: sickness, the onset of death, persecution by an enemy, betrayal by a friend and enforced separation from the sanctuary of God are among them. Sometimes it's simply not possible to be sure what lies behind the psalmist's cry for help. What is clear, however, is that these psalms are desperate for a 'hearing'. And the knowledge that God hears the sufferer's cry for help almost always turns the psalm round from lament to hope and even thanksgiving.

The psalm laments are among the profoundest texts on the theme of suffering in the Bible, or indeed anywhere. They rank with the Servant Songs of Isaiah, the laments of Jeremiah and the book of Job for their insight into pain and what it means to have faith in YHWH in the midst of it. There is no pretending that pain is not real and terrible, no fantasy that religion will somehow do away with it or ease it. The psalm that Jesus quotes makes it clear that what the sufferer is going through brings him to the very edge of what a human being can endure:

> Save me, O God,
> > for the waters have come up to my neck.
> I sink in deep mire,
> > where there is no foothold;
> I have come into deep waters,
> > and the flood sweeps over me.
> I am weary with my crying;
> > my throat is parched.
> My eyes grow dim
> > with waiting for my God.
>
> More in number than the hairs of my head
> > are those who hate me without cause;
> many are those who would destroy me,
> > my enemies who accuse me falsely . . .
>
> Do not let the flood sweep over me,
> > or the deep swallow me up,
> > or the Pit close its mouth over me . . .
> You know the insults I receive,
> > and my shame and dishonour;
> > my foes are all known to you.
> Insults have broken my heart,

> so that I am in despair.
> I looked for pity, but there was none;
>   and for comforters, but I found none.
> They gave me poison for food,
>   and for my thirst they gave me vinegar to drink.
>
> (Psalms 69.1–4, 15, 19–21)

One of the themes of the Passion Narrative is that Jesus fulfils the destiny of this lonely sufferer. We have already seen how he is the true 'Israel' who acts out the vocation his people had failed to fulfil in their long and wayward history. But here the emphasis is more on Jesus as the archetypal suffering human being. As the man who suffers, who is not spared the pain that is part of the human condition, he is every-man, every child of Adam. 'When the New Testament hears the laments in Jesus' voice, this is not simply a prophetic and messianic move . . . This means that all the cries for help that have come forth and still come forth from human lips, all the laments that we have uttered and will utter, are taken up on the laments of Christ' (Miller, 2005, p. 20). When Pilate brings Jesus out of the praetorium he announces to the crowd and to the world, 'Here is the man!'(19.5): *ecce homo*, the embodiment of all that it means to be mortal and fulfil the destiny of a human being. His is 'Son of Man' because of his regalia: the purple robe and crown of thorns. But we also recognize him as 'man' because of the marks of his suffering. This man of sorrows identifies himself with the nameless sufferer in the psalm, who is both a specific human being, yet any human being at any time, anywhere.

We have talked about the link between passion and compassion. The Passion Narrative, like the laments, is a text that tests how far we have developed the Christian ability to 'suffer with'. One of the classic devotions connected with the passion familiar to many Christians is known as the Stations of the Cross. This is a sequence of fourteen images of the passion of Jesus displayed on the walls of Roman Catholic (and some Anglican) churches. They originated as a way of substituting for pilgrimage to the holy sites associated with the passion in Jerusalem. If you couldn't walk the *Via Dolorosa* itself, then you could walk it in your local church.

The Stations take us inside the story through imaginative meditation and prayer so that we can become participants in the passion rather than mere observers. Some of its forms are undeniably debased and pander to a sentimental piety of 'feeling sorry for Jesus', emphatically not what the passion is about. But we should not deny the importance of learning to read the passion in a way that concentrates not only on what Jesus has done for us but also on how we ourselves *respond* to this image of suffering displayed so vividly before us. The Stations can help us to be 'present' to the events whose story we tell, and in particular, become sensitized to pain. This helps us develop the art of compassionate engagement. If we can learn to read the passion in that way, maybe we can also learn to read the pain of the world with compassion too. I wrote earlier of my experience watching the film *The Passion of the Christ*. What gave it special poignancy was watching another film next day. *Fahrenheit 9/11* is a documentary indictment of American foreign policy in recent years. It memorably showed the suffering of Iraqi civilians as a result of the US intervention of 2003. Their terrible suffering on the same screen as the one where I had watched Christ's terrible suffering the day before made a connection that could only be turned into compassion and prayer.

In 2000, on a pilgrimage to Jerusalem, I visited the holocaust memorial of Yad Vashem. I wanted to do this to pay my respects to members of my grandmother's and mother's family who had perished in Nazi extermination camps. I tried to express my thoughts in a diary entry at the time:

> I go first to the children's memorial. From the fierce sunshine, I am plunged into darkness and grope around, disorientated, looking for something to hold on to. There are a million candle lights all around, as if I were floating among the stars, and I can't yet work out which are reflections and which are real. A disembodied voice reads the names of child victims of

the Sho'ah while dolorous music seems to emerge from the depths of the grave itself. It is theatrically brilliant (I am ashamed to say I have the usual aesthetic reaction) but not at the cost of authenticity. No one could fail to be moved by this place and the thoughts it evokes. I feel I want to stay here until all the names have been read – that it would be an insult to any one of these holy innocents not to hear their name pronounced and for me to utter what prayer I can. Reluctantly, I stumble outside into the light.

There is a sudden silence here that is in stark contrast to the noise of old Jerusalem. Everyone walks alone here: no one wishes to talk. I go next to the exhibition of the holocaust, with its unforgettable images of life under national socialism. A photograph of dead and dying children on the pavements of the Warsaw Ghetto affects me deeply. How could this happen in my beloved Europe? How could the hearts of even the most hardened SS officers not bleed? In the memorial hall, a steward asks me to cover my head. An eternal flame burns there, amid the names of the death camps sculpted on the floor. This too is a holy place where perhaps the only texts to read are the book of Job and the Passion Narrative. I pray as best I can, but it is hard to ask for anything, least of all forgiveness. It is numbing to be here. It strips you of your ability to speak, even to think, for there is nothing to say.

A Christian at Yad Vashem inevitably thinks of Jesus the Jewish sufferer at the hands of a Roman *Reich*, especially if he or she has just walked the *Via Dolorosa* in the old city. Theology draws on the imagery of 'holocaust' in its attempts to interpret the cross as a sacrifice. Some of this theologizing is highly problematic. But Jesus as the victim on whom the *Reich* had no mercy takes us toward the heart of how we should view undeserved pain. For if the thirsting Jesus is an emblem of a human being in distress, every human being in distress is an emblem of the crucified Jesus. A *theologia crucis* that has nothing to say about suffering human-

ity simply has nothing to say. But if the passion is allowed to illuminate the human experience of pain, our response to it is raised
to an altogether different level.

I mean by this that if, instead of speaking about the 'problem' of
suffering we talked about the *mystery* of it, we would begin to see
how the passion is an icon not only of the mystery of suffering, but
also of the mystery of love. In other words, the cross stands for the
meeting of the two profoundest mysteries of our existence. Love is
no more susceptible to intellectual apprehension than suffering;
the 'problem' of love's origin and meaning is as unanswerable as the
'problem' of suffering. But to embrace a contemplative spirituality
of the passion is to begin to intuit how the mysteries of love and
pain belong together. They meet in the cross; and because the cross
is the archetypal, universal symbol of the human being presented to
God, they can begin to meet in the experience of the world as well,
and in the way we ourselves respond to its suffering.

As I emerged silenced and shaken from Yad Vashem, a group of
children was arriving. I wondered whether they were prepared for
what they were about to experience. But then I had not been prepared for what I saw either, and perhaps it is better that way. Their
enjoyment of a day out of school might have signified callousness
or indifference. Or maybe it hinted at the light that bathes the
cross in St John's story.

Israeli school children are brought to Yad Vashem to learn of
the dark night experienced by their people. Yet the ebullience
of youth, in a free society, prevents them from being over-
whelmed by the horror. On the lawns near the waiting buses
they soon are engaged in the typical play activities of young
people the world over. Nearby is a piece of sculpture: a large
anonymous mother figure. Her outstretched arms clasp life-
less figures of children. Here is a strange convergence: the
national memorial to the victims of the Holocaust, in the
newly reborn state of Israel, the dark shadow that the Shoah
casts, beneath the usually sun-lit sky, the memory of one and

one-half murdered children, and the laughter of living Israeli children.   (Eckardt and Eckardt, 1988, p. 220)

The way Psalm 69 is quoted bears on this. In full the psalm says: 'They gave me poison for food, and for my thirst they gave me vinegar to drink.' This is part of a larger section in which the psalmist berates those who are persecuting him. It is immediately followed by one of the notorious 'curses' that call down the wrath of heaven: 'Let their eyes be darkened so that they cannot see . . . Pour out your indignation upon them, and let your burning anger overtake them . . . Let them be blotted out of the book of the living' (Psalms 69.23, 24, 28).

But Jesus quotes none of this. In the Passion Narrative, this bitter hatred of the enemy is not even hinted at. It's as if St John wants us to see in the cross how hatred is absorbed by the suffering of *this* righteous victim. This has already become clear in the garden in Jesus' word to Peter. It becomes even clearer in the praetorium where we learn that his kingdom is 'not from this world'. There we learned how hatred lies behind all violence. But now we can see what God's answer to hatred is. By the time we get to the cross, we understand how this story is about a friend laying down his life for his friends. In this transfiguration, the old is overtaken by the new. So it's not simply that vengefulness has no place at Golgotha (which is Luke's message), more that at this place and this hour it is utterly and finally transfigured by the light and glory of God's grace and truth revealed in this last and greatest sign of all.

*   *   *

What this place and this 'hour' mean for St John is a theme we have already encountered in the Passion Narrative. We saw, in the garden, that Jesus spoke of his God-given vocation to suffer and die. 'Am I not to drink the cup that the Father has given me?' Now, on the cross, his 'hour' has arrived, and it is time to drink the 'cup'.

And once again in the Passion Narrative, Jesus' word about his thirst, and the cup that he must drink, evoke the memory of an episode earlier in John's story.

It's not the first time Jesus has been thirsty in the Gospel. There has been another occasion, an age ago it must have seemed, when Jesus has asked for a drink from a stranger. It was the same time of day as the hour of his crucifixion, 'about noon' (19.14), the time when shadows are shortest and the sun's glare fiercest. The Gospel's first recorded thirst (if we don't count the rather different kind of thirst at Cana) is at Jacob's well at Sychar in Samaria. Jesus is tired out by his journey. A Samaritan woman comes to draw water. He asks her to draw some out for him. During the extended dialogue that follows, Jesus tells her that he himself will be a source that will quench her thirst for ever. 'Lord, give me this water, so that I may never be thirsty again' she says. And at the end of the story, when Jesus has disclosed to the Samaritans who he is, they find their faith bursting out of them, like water from a spring: 'We have heard for ourselves, and we know that this is truly the Saviour of the world' (4.1–42).

This encounter is beautifully handled by St John. One of its timeless contributions to the Christian tradition is the honour and courtesy that Jesus accords to a woman. But it's all part of a story designed to show how need is turned into gift. What Jesus needs is water from the well. Yet that is precisely what he goes on to offer a woman whose thirst is deeper and more desperate than she can know. And, as so often in the Gospel, what is offered to Jesus as the raw material for him to work with is given back enriched and transformed. Like the wine at the wedding feast, and the loaves that feed the crowd, a pitcher of water from the well is transmuted into a vast river welling up to eternal life and healing everything it touches.

All of this is being recalled by Jesus' word *dipso*. John is saying that it is the same on the cross as it was at Jacob's well. The crucified Lord is a human being on whom all but the hardest hearted would look with some degree of compassion. Once again, he is tired out by the journey that has led here, not only from the upper room, not only from Galilee but from heaven itself. It is for this, he has told Pilate, that he has made the journey into this world; and now he has reached his final destination. There is no darkness over the cross in St John, so crucifixion under the midday sun would have wrung every drop of moisture out of the tortured body of Jesus. The moistening of his lips echoes his thirst quenched at the well. But the tables are turned once again: need becomes gift. Once again, Jesus' thirst means the quenching of other people's thirsts, indeed, the thirst of an entire world. John might have said that this was to fulfil what Jesus had said once before: 'Let anyone who is thirsty come to me, and let the one who believes in me drink. As the scripture has said, "Out of the believer's heart shall flow rivers of living water"' (7.37–8).

The cross, then, is that well from which living water flows out to the whole world. There is another seam of Old Testament reference here. One of the prophets looks forward to the day when 'living waters shall flow out from Jerusalem' (Zechariah 14.8) while another has a vision of the glorious temple from which a life-giving river flows out to refresh and renew the entire world (Ezekiel 47.1–12). This is another aspect of the complex symbolism of the blood and water that flow out of Jesus' side, symbols of life exchanged, his thirst for our quenching, his wounds for our healing, his life laid down for ours given back to us.

*   *   *

But it isn't only Jesus who has thirsts. In the previous chapter I said something about love-as-desire. Let me return to the theme of our own human needs and how the cross interprets them.

In the context of the First Word, I wrote of people who embark on pilgrimage as a way of challenging the values of a consumerist society. The need to 'possess' has to be a major disease of our modern affluence. There is probably no single underlying cause for people's addiction to it, but a major factor must be unconscious needs such as emptiness and *ennui*, and the craving for satisfaction and fulfilment. In a penetrating study of consumerism, one writer whose theme is the 'goods' of consumerism concludes that

shopping, which seems so much a part of our external, social
existence, often refers back to our internal world. Shopping frequently provides a pleasurable but temporary substitute for a
sense of identity. We may shop as a means to repairing and
transforming unacceptable aspects of our identities or to the
delivery of longed-for aspects of the self. (Minsky, 2000, p. 51)

This almost theological language is a good comment on how consumerism reveals the void left behind by the ebbing of religious faith.
The 'spirituality of gratitude' that I proposed earlier would show us
how the 'goods' of the gospel meet the needs that runaway material-
ism tries to address: gratitude tells the truth about where 'benefit'
really lies. One implication of it will be a reappraisal of the material
world and our part in it. To be thankful for the goodness of creation
is to respond to it not out of the need to dominate or possess but out
of a sense of privileged responsibility and ethical awareness.

How do the 'goods' of the gospel meet human need? Augustine
is the West's supreme theologian of human desire. His *Confessions*
is one of the greatest testaments to the life-changing power of
Christianity ever penned. We tend to blame Augustine for many
of the ills of the Western church, not least in the area of sexuality.
Yet here is a man who understood the ebbs and flows of desire and
longing, and who came to see how the gospel is God's answer to
the hungers and thirsts that surge up within the human soul.

Only a believer who had lived this in his own experience could
have written the timeless affirmation of gratitude and love with
which the book opens: 'You have made us for yourself, and our
heart is restless until it rests in you' (Augustine, 1992, Book I, i (1)
p. 3). He understands the seduction of desire that is focused on
the world, and how this very desire points to his own emptiness
and need of God:

Late have I loved you, beauty so old and so new: late have I
loved you. And see, you were within and I was in the external
world and sought you there, and in my unlovely state

I plunged into those lovely created things which you made. You were with me, and I was not with you. The lovely things kept me far from you, though if they did not have their existence in you, they would have no existence at all. You called and cried out loud and shattered my deafness. You were radiant and resplendent, you put to flight my blindness. You were fragrant, and I drew in my breath and now pant after you. I tasted you, and I feel but hunger and thirst for you. You touched me, and I am set on fire to attain the peace which is yours.   (Augustine, 1992, Book X, xxvii (38), p. 201)

We are struck by Augustine's highly sensual way of speaking where his 'passion', far from being repressed, is channelled into his discovery of God – or rather God's discovery of him. He does not see his conflicted past as the absence of love but as love that was disordered and misdirected. This gives him the freedom to use powerfully physical language to describe his longing for God. He is the absent friend for whom his soul is in torment. He has pierced his heart with the arrow of love as if Christ were a heavenly Eros. All his human hungers and thirsts are poured into his love for God:

When I love you, what is it that I love? It is not physical beauty nor temporal glory nor the brightness of light dear to earthly eyes, nor the sweet melodies of all kinds of songs, nor the gentle odour of flowers and ointments and perfumes, nor manna or honey, nor limbs welcoming the embraces of the flesh: it is not these I love when I love my God. Yet there is a light I love, and a food, and a kind of embrace when I love my God – a light, voice, odour, food, embrace, of my inner man, where my soul is floodlit by light which space cannot contain, where there is sound that time cannot seize, where there is a perfume which no breeze disperses, where there is a taste for food no amount of eating can lessen, and where there is a bond of union that no satiety can part. That is what I love when I love my God.   (Augustine, 1992, Book X, vi (8), p. 183)

This language about God as the Being in whom all desires and longings come together is close to John's spirituality of desire and longing. At the beginning of this chapter I suggested that John's Jesus is not aloof from ordinary human needs. He tells us that we can make friends of our desires because, in coming to meet us, Jesus both acknowledges and transfigures them. So many stories in his Gospel can be read this way: Cana in Galilee, the feeding of the crowd, the man born blind, the raising of Lazarus, all point to frustrated human need and how Jesus meets and transforms it. This Seventh Word and the story it recalls is a case in point *par excellence*: the woman at the well whose disordered desires were positively Augustinian in scale. Yet she came to realize the God-shaped thirst within her and how it could be quenched for ever in Jesus the Living Water.

So this word from the cross turns out not only to express a need but to issue an invitation. We 'behold the man', and we see ourselves in him, needy, thirsty, suffering; yet now healed, ennobled, transfigured. Because Jesus has been thirsty and drunk the cup held out to him, we can come to him and drink, and find that hope is born, together with a sense of relief, not unlike the quenching of thirst, that we have mercifully not been allowed to have the last word on our own desires and destinies.

It's the great mystery of Good Friday that it is for us that Jesus thirsts: for every human being, and for the world itself. Christian devotion and gratitude are focused on the knowledge that it is for us that he hangs on the cross. We cannot add anything to his work, only receive at his hands the cup which this time is not filled with sour wine but with the richest and best vintage the true Vine can give us. As we take that cup, we find our God-given destiny and our own deepest happiness. Our destiny may not turn out to be what we dreamed of, but we know that the hands of the crucified Jesus point us to a reality that keeps us safe. He bears witness to the truth not only of God but our own selves. At Golgotha, illusions are stripped away and we are known for what we are. Beyond Golgotha, a promise beckons: and we glimpse through resurrection what we shall become.

The Eighth Word

John 19.30

⇒◆⇐

'It is finished.'

The Last Word is about endings – and beginnings.

We have seen how the four Gospels give us very different sayings with which Jesus takes his leave of the world. In Matthew and Mark the last words from the cross are desperate, God-forsaken and stark: 'My God, my God, why have you abandoned me?' In Luke, they are confident and trusting: 'Father, into your hands I commend my spirit.' And in John, they are different again: 'It is finished.'

Like the Seventh Word, this final saying is a single word in the Greek: *tetelestai*. But what does it mean? And more than that, how are we meant to *hear* it? I have heard it read many times on Good Friday as if it were a sigh of resignation or defeat, the last whisper of a dying man who has given up on life. We perhaps see our own mortality that way and read it into the text: whoever we are, whatever we have done, death is the great leveller. *Memento mori.* When it's over, it's over, finished, gone.

In Bach's *St John Passion*, the words are set to a motif that seems to fall to the ground and die. The musical phrase echoes the bow of the head with which John says Jesus 'gives up his spirit'. Does Bach mean it to die away into nothing? It's usually sung that way. But this cannot be right given the contralto movement that immediately follows it. It begins as one of those poignantly beautiful arias at which Bach excelled where the soul meditates on the mystery of death and draws comfort from the words 'It is accomplished.' But Bach suddenly interrupts this serene atmosphere with a stirring victory song: 'The hero of Judah wins with triumph and ends the fight.' Bach's message is that while death is indeed 'the last enemy', *this* death marks the beginning of the great reversal through which life is given back to the world. This means that the singer who takes his leave of the work with this all-important bar somehow has to marry the fall of the musical phrase to the rise of spiritual hope and the expectation of triumph. It calls for musicianship of the highest order.

Bach, a devout Lutheran, was a keen student of the Bible. Few composers have equalled his ability to immerse himself in biblical texts and illuminate their meaning through music. Albert Schweitzer, to whom scholars both of Bach and of the New Testament owe so much, said that 'if we have once absorbed a biblical verse in Bach's setting of it, we can never again conceive it in any other rhythm' (Schweitzer, 1923, vol. II, p. 27). He calls this gift of making the music not only memorable but inevitable the 'power of persistence'. Words on a page can't begin to do justice to it: we need to listen to the music and allow it to inform the way we read the text. Music, like poetry, literature and art, has a place in the interpretation of the Bible. Bach deserves to be heard and studied as a theologian in his own right, with his own insights into the meaning of the scriptures. His *Passion* stands as one of the great post-Reformation commentaries on St John.

So this last word is much more than the mere acknowledgement that Jesus' life has come to an end. It's striking that in the space of three short verses the Greek word 'to accomplish' is used no fewer than three times. 'After this, when Jesus knew that all was now accomplished, he said, in order to accomplish the scripture, "I thirst".' Then comes the last cry itself: 'It is accomplished.' The first and third occurrences are identical: *tetelestai*. In all three cases, the word carries the sense of things moving purposefully to their appointed conclusion. At the climax of the narrative, John is at pains to underline yet again that all of this was meant. The story has its 'teleology'.

If we have followed St John, we once again hear powerful echoes from earlier in the Gospel. As so often, an apparently trivial incident becomes the occasion to underline a truth about the work of Jesus. It is folded into the story that we looked at in the previous chapter, Jesus' meeting with the Samaritan woman. The disciples are urging Jesus to eat something. He replies: 'I have food to eat that you do not know about.' They conjecture what his secret provision might be, just as the woman has conjectured about the kind of drink Jesus has mysteriously alluded to. Then Jesus says: 'My food is to do the will of him who sent me and to complete his work' (4.34). There, the thirst of Jesus is followed by his speaking about completing the task his Father has given him. On the cross, it's the same: 'I thirst' is answered by 'It is accomplished.' John's meaning is unmistakable: that Jesus' hunger and thirst to do God's will are finally satisfied as he gives up his spirit and dies.

But we need to look back even further than this. An ending implies a beginning: a *telos* needs an *archē*. What could this beginning be? The answer is found at the very outset of the Gospel: 'In the beginning was the Word' (1.1). The last word of Jesus answers the first word of John's book. St John is saying that the man who has spoken finally from the cross is none other than the same Word who at the dawn of time spoke into the dark and formless void and called the *cosmos* into being.

John clearly has the creation story in mind at the cross. It is Friday, the sixth day of the Hebrew week. In the creation story at the beginning of the book of Genesis, it's at the end of the sixth day that 'the heavens and the earth were finished . . . And on the seventh day God finished the work that he had done' (Genesis 2.1–2). The word used in the Greek translation of the Hebrew Bible, the Septuagint familiar to John's readers, is a close relative of *tetelestai*. The inference is obvious. Just as, in the mythological chronology of Genesis the work of creation was completed at the end of the first week, so on the cross another work of creation has been 'accomplished'. Humanity, the world, the entire *cosmos* has been remade. There is nothing more to do. The crucified Creator may now rest on the seventh day from all the work that he has done. So he bows his head and hands over his spirit.

*   *   *

The last word on the cross announces the destiny of the great 'I AM' of Israel whom Jesus has identified himself with in the First Word. The act of creation and the history that flows from it has all been leading up to this moment. Now, for the last time, John reminds us through the one word *tetelestai* how the cross has been the intended 'end' of Jesus' career. Jesus takes up this same word near the beginning of his prayer before the passion. Linked with it is another of John's key words: 'I *glorified* you on earth by *finishing* the work that you gave me to do' (17.4). These two ideas of *accomplishment* and *glory*, taken together, are vital to understanding the cross in St John.

There is a well-known saying by Sir Francis Drake that is based on this Eighth Word. In endeavouring any great matter, he says, 'There must be a beginning of any great matter, but the continuing unto the end until it be thoroughly finished yields the true glory.' It's no doubt good – even glorious – to be a 'completer-finisher' as well as an initiator and shaper, not just in great matters but small ones too. But it's not what John means. We need to go back to the prologue of his Gospel to grasp this, and revisit once more the word we looked at in connection with the signs that run through the Gospel from Cana to the cross. That word is 'glory'.

For John, 'glory' is not so much an idea as a person. In a story in the Hebrew Bible, Moses prays that he might see God's glory. He learns that the sight of God's face would be too much for him: it would kill him (Exodus 33.18–20) just as the sight of Zeus's splendour killed Semele who was foolish enough to ask to see it.

But the magnificent message of St John is that the incarnate Word has revealed precisely what Moses longed to see, the Father's glory. 'We have seen his glory . . . full of grace and truth' (1.14). The Gospel spells out what this means. Glory, says John, is disclosed as Jesus bears witness to the truth and lives out the love of his Father. For love is another of those words that is also directly associated with Jesus' goal or *telos*, what he must accomplish in obedience to his Father's will. John introduces the account of the washing of feet by saying: 'Jesus knew that his hour had come to depart from this world and go to the Father. Having loved his own who were in the world, he loved them to the end' (13.1): *eis telon* in the Greek. The 'end' is what is reached and accomplished in the cry *tetelestai*. For John, the true glory of God is in the finished work of Jesus because in his death, when his hour is here, love's work is complete.

There is a complex and fascinating cluster of meanings and associations here: 'accomplished', 'glory', 'hour', 'truth' and 'love'. The text is undeniably very dense with concentrated meanings, but it's how John writes: many resonances are set off by his use of single words. In the music of Wagner, a few bars of music, a brief phrase, even a single chord can evoke an association to a particular character or object, recall a complex event, paint an emotional mood. The leitmotif is a trigger or clue that encapsulates in a few moments of music what it would take several minutes to explain in words. John's 'leading motifs' that texture the Gospel have the same effect: they trigger a rich array of resonances that play across the Gospel like light falling on silk. Jesus' word *tetelestai* sends us back through the Gospel to rediscover how St John has been telling of glory, service, truth and love all along. What was foreshadowed before is now brought out into the clear light of day. *Tetelestai* means what it means because of where it is uttered. The cross brings out the ultimate depths hidden in these words, and tells us how they are gathered up in what Jesus has accomplished.

For John, this most numinous moment in history is a demonstration of power that marks the final unveiling of the person of Jesus the Messiah. We have seen how power has coloured the Passion Narrative. John presents us with the paradox of the man who has renounced power, indeed has become the victim of it, and yet retains throughout the ordeal of the passion a regal dignity that speaks of a kingdom 'not from here'. And on the cross, where the crucified man is reduced to complete powerlessness, St John tells us that he is at his most noble and majestic. Indeed, the place where he is 'lifted up' is nothing less than a throne. The Passion Narrative, the entire Gospel, is leading up to this point. Pilate's jibe 'So you are a king then!', the purple robe, the crown of thorns, the title over the cross, the mocking of the crowd, all these ironies turn out to proclaim the truth. The messianic dreams and hopes of the centuries have come true. Israel has her long-awaited King! And not just Israel, but the world.

The paradoxes of triumph-in-humility in the reign of the servant-king on his cross have been celebrated in some of the best hymns of the passion. One of the most famous, *Vexilla Regis*, by the seventh-century Bishop of Poitiers, Venantius Fortunatus, was incorporated as an office hymn into the liturgy of Passiontide. It is thoroughly imbued with Johannine thought and imagery, though the English translation hardly does justice to the beautiful Latin poem:

> Fulfilled is all that David told
> In true prophetic song of old,
> The universal Lord is he,
> Who reigns and triumphs from the tree.
>
> O tree of beauty, tree of light,
> O tree with royal purple dight,
> Elect on whose triumphal breast
> Those holy limbs should find their rest!

The joyful triumphant tone that runs through this text could not be further removed from the gloomy piety of Good Friday fostered by such nineteenth-century hymns as 'O come and mourn with me a while'. The seventeenth-century German hymnwriter Paul Gerhardt has an acute sensitivity to the pain and agony of the passion, but he never loses sight of the majesty of the suffering Jesus:

> O sacred head, sore wounded,
> Defiled and put to scorn;
> O kingly head, surrounded
> With mocking crown of thorn:
> What sorrow mars thy grandeur?
> Can death thy bloom deflower?
> O countenance whose splendour
> The hosts of heaven adore.

The most famous English hymn of the passion by the seventeenth-century Isaac Watts breathes the same atmosphere of crucified nobility that makes us wonder when we sing it how anything else could possibly compete with the cross for our longing, desire and devotion:

> When I survey the wondrous cross
> On which the Prince of glory died,
> My richest gain I count but loss,
> And pour contempt on all my pride.

And from our own time comes an imaginative interpretation of the kingship of Jesus that beautifully echoes John's theme of sacrificial love:

> Therefore he who shows us God
> helpless hangs upon a tree;
> and the nails and crown of thorns
> tell of what God's love must be.
>
> Here is God: no monarch he,
> throned in easy state to reign;
> here is God, whose arms of love,
> aching, spent, the world sustain.
>
> (Vanstone, 1979, pp. 119–20)

The insight is that kingship, as Jesus exemplifies it, comes with a price that is infinitely high. That is the laying down of life as the ultimate expression of self-giving. For the author of that hymn, how Jesus reigns from the cross is no different from how God always reigns as King. The cross is iconic of God's sovereignty. Therefore it must define our entire understanding, not only of the passion, but of Christianity itself.

*   *   *

I say this because of what I see to be a major threat facing Christianity in our time. It comes not from the external challenges posed by secularism or the ascendancy of other religious communities in a mixed society. It's an internal threat that has to do with our understanding of the gospel itself: what we truly believe about God and how we speak about him 'before the world'. If I am right about the Eight Passion Words, then they raise very key questions about how we bear witness to this King of Glory. Christians naturally want to testify to God's kingship. It's abundantly clear from all four Gospels that kingship was fundamental to Jesus' understanding of himself and his mission. But we have seen how the language of kingly power can betray assumptions that easily get translated into actions that are not only misguided but dangerous.

We have seen how kingship in St John is subtly nuanced and infinitely carefully handled. The threat to Christianity, as I see it, is that this gets displaced by a kind of triumphalism with its crude expectation that God's reign will restore truth and right wrongs by an act of *force majeure.* This is the disfiguring theology that led to the Crusades. But the tendency is still with us. Some popular worship songs are highly coloured by hopes and longings – even the belief – that God will decisively intervene in history in a way that will be unambiguously recognized by the whole world. When we sing 'Shine, Jesus, shine, fill this land with the Father's glory', is this the language of metaphor, spiritual aspiration or literal expectation? You could sing it in front of the crucifix, or kneeling before the blessed sacrament, or on a 'praise march' round the city and mean very different things by it. What would St John mean?

Helen Orchard warns that 'Jesus' "hour of glory" is not his "glorious hour", with all the brassy, triumphalist overtones conveyed by that term. Instead it is the hour of liberation through *pathos.* Salvation is mediated through the internment, torture and immolation of the victim of God' (Orchard, 1998, p. 247). Terry Eagleton, the cultural historian and literary critic, says:

> . . . only by accepting the worst for what it is, not as a convenient springboard for leaping beyond it, can one hope to surpass it. Only by accepting this as the last word about the human condition can it cease to be the last word . . . It was precisely this bereftness, savoured to the last bitter drop, which in a classically tragic rhythm could then become the source of renewed life . . . The destitute condition of humanity, if it was to be fully restored, had to be lived all the way through, pressed to the extreme limit of a descent into the hell of meaninglessness and desolation, rather than disavowed, patched-up or short-circuited.   (Eagleton, 2003, p. 27)

Tetelestai in St John is a cry of royal triumph. But only at the cost of abasement, taking to its farthest limits what had been implicit when he had washed his disciples' feet. In a famous New Testament poem where St Paul seems at his closest to St John, the career of Jesus is pictured as a magnificent movement of God out towards the world. 'Though he was in the form of God, did not regard equality with God as something to be exploited, but emptied himself, taking the form of a slave, being born in human likeness. And being found in human form, he humbled himself and became obedient to the point of death – even death on a cross' (Philippians 2.6–8). This grand drama has heaven and earth in awe. But in St John, this triumphant event does not issue in dramatic convulsions of nature like an eclipse of the sun or an earthquake, or even the veil of the temple being torn apart as in other

Gospels. In John's story, people go about the business that always follows death: identifying a tomb, preparing the body for burial, supporting one another. And starting to believe.

St John offers only two pieces of evidence that the world has been changed because of what Jesus has done. Like so much in the Gospel, they seem unpromising material on which to base a large claim. The first is in the action of Jesus at his death. He bows his head and 'hands over his spirit'. We came across the word *paradidōmi* earlier in this book, when we saw how the entire passion story is a sequence of 'handings over'. Now, Jesus bequeaths his spirit to God and to the church, symbolized by Mary and John at the foot of the cross. They are the firstborn in the community of truth and love that originates here at Golgotha.

The second piece of evidence is in what the soldier does. He pierces the side of the dead Jesus, and blood and water flow out. John takes this to be deeply symbolic of what the cross represents: 'He who saw this has testified so that you also may believe' (19.35). We have already seen that this means the life and love of Jesus flowing out to the world: living water to quench its thirst, wine with which to celebrate the marriage of heaven and earth.

Of course, we can't leave Easter out of this: St John would not allow us to read the passion story without the resurrection that follows. And his resurrection story is entirely of a piece with the passion. For St John, the evidence of Jesus' triumph is not found in dramatic displays of power so much as in the transformation of those who believe in him. The resurrection is not heralded by a fanfare of trumpets. Indeed, whereas the passion is presented as an event of cosmic significance, the resurrection has an almost hidden quality about it. The disciples and Mary Magdalen in the garden, the Eleven in the upper room, even the climax of Thomas' acclamation of Jesus as Lord and God, all seem to happen in a place apart, unseen by the world. There is no triumphalism here. The text is reticent about so much that surrounds the new era that begins at Easter except for one thing: how people respond to it. Faith, love, obedience – these are the marks of citizenship in Jesus' kingdom.

All this is to say that the vocation to be a Christian in the world is both exhilarating and testing. Life is messy, complex and difficult, and the temptation has always been to take the easy path of early closures and swift resolutions. Faith is the demanding assignment to learn to read the world *sub specie crucis*, under the perspective of the cross, irradiated by the kingship of Jesus in his passion and resurrection. In that light, things begin to look different. So our responses begin to be different too. We learn to live with complexity and stay with tough issues, not because it is easy but because persevering faith requires and allows it. We learn the virtue of patience, which is to wait until God's time for disclosure has come. And because we are humble before the human facts of our condition and the divine facts of the cross and resurrection, we begin to know our place. Here are the seeds of a spirituality for our times that we can be grateful to be taught by the profound and wise author of the Fourth Gospel.

*   *   *

In this book I have tried to show how the Eight Words of the passion enlarge our understanding of the cross. We have seen how they embrace our search for meaning, address the perennial issues of power and violence, define truth and love, shed light on the nature of community and personal relationships, interpret suffering, meet our desires, set out a vision for the church. They are concerned about the large and small things of life. The 'big picture' asks questions about the kind of world we live in, a world in which the same injustices and abuses that crucified Jesus continue to be perpetrated against innocent victims. But this is not at the expense of the individual, personal questions the cross puts to us about our integrity as men and women, our witness to 'truth', our care for others, what it means to follow Jesus with gratitude, how to love.

The final Word elevates all of this to a universal plane. It's easy to use the word 'cosmic' rhetorically and mean by it little more than 'big' or 'impressive'. But I want deliberately to echo St John's language here. We have seen how *cosmos* is a key word in the Fourth Gospel; indeed, St John uses it in his Gospel and letters more than any other New Testament writer. Often he means the 'world' that is hostile to God, subject to the destructive influences of sin and death. But in a more basic sense, it means the created order itself, not simply the 'world' of humanity but nothing less than the universe in all its vastness and diversity. For John, this *cosmos* has been the theatre of God's activity since the beginning when the Word spoke and there was light. Into this universe, because of God's great love, Jesus has come unknown and unrecognized. He is the 'Lamb of God who takes away the sin of the world!' (1.29). In St John's vision, incarnation and cross are one story, one event: Jesus making his home within the *cosmos*, and re-creating it through an act that draws all things together into reconciliation and unity. His perspective on what Jesus has 'accomplished' is that it is the defining moment not only of human history but in the history of the universe.

'Spirituality' is always tempted to be preoccupied with the immediate concerns of our personal lives and relationships. Of course, this aspect of what we are features strongly in John's account of the cross; at one level, this is what Mary and John represent at Golgotha. But the Eighth Word's cry of accomplishment raises our sights to a different plane as well. For the cross stands above us as the ultimate confrontation between what John calls 'light' and 'darkness', the power of love taking on the power of destructiveness and evil. Something of this is captured in Salvador Dali's well-known painting of the crucified Jesus hanging in space above planet earth – a very Johannine image. Or in the words that Christopher Marlowe puts into the mouth of Faust, 'See, see, where Christ's blood streams in the firmament!'

What might it mean to say that the crucifixion is as decisive an event for the universe as the Big Bang or some other singularity in the unfolding story of the cosmos? The possibility of extra-terrestrial intelligence, and how this fits in our world-view is not just a matter for cosmologists. Many theologians are intensely interested in it, and in the implications that alien life forms would have for our understanding of God and of ourselves in a purposeful universe. These possibilities become even more intriguing if we admit, as many cosmologists do, that our universe may be part of a 'multiverse' in which other universes exist in parallel with ours but in different dimensions of space and time.

These questions are not the Fourth Gospel's of course. Yet I dare to think that a book whose opening words envision the entire order of space and time being in relationship with the Word cannot but have in view a salvation with a scope that is just as universal. So I believe we hear the Eighth Word spoken not only to the human race but to all creation. If *tetelestai* answers 'In the beginning', then it answers a cosmic and not simply a human story. What is 'accomplished' might have nuances related to God's responsibility for the cost of the evolutionary process in the cosmos, or his identifying with every creature that experiences pain, whether intelligent or not, or with the eventual fulfilment of the universe's *telos*, as yet only partially realized.

If the cross is, literally, the *crux* of history, the hinge on which everything turns, the once-for-all event that gathers everything up into itself, then its implications do not belong to our planet alone. Whatever salvation may mean on other worlds, if we follow St John its meaning for us will be a paradigm of God's purpose in re-making creation according to his purpose of love. Something of this is hinted at in the letter to the Colossians, where in a magnificent passage Paul speaks of Christ as 'the image of the invisible God, the firstborn of all creation' and goes on to tell how, through him, 'God was pleased to reconcile to himself all things, whether on earth or in heaven, by making peace through the blood of his cross' (Colossians 1.15ff.). In John, *tetelestai* is the cry of triumph that reverberates across the universe and across all aeons. What myriad worlds in times to come will hear it and rejoice?

How this vast vision of the cross is realized in our world and in our own experience is something we can only discover as we place ourselves within the Passion Narrative and begin to live it. Now that we have read this far, we know that the cross forms and informs everything we are. We cannot be Christians unless we live a 'cruciform' spirituality. That means being before God and the world in a way that is genuinely open to the transforming possibilities we have explored: the truth that exposes falsehood, the love that absorbs hatred, the intimacy that overcomes separation, the humility that teaches us our place in the world, the gratitude that frees us from disordered desire.

This is the end of the journey that began in the garden when Jesus asked, 'Whom do you seek?' We now know why in the English-speaking world we call the day of the cross Good Friday. In other countries it is 'holy'. To us it is simply 'good'. It's a title John would have loved. The day of painful things is good because of the Eighth Word. The King of Glory reigns. The new creation can come into being. Love has triumphed.

*　　　*　　　*

The Passion Narrative ends as it began, in a garden. All is accomplished. It only remains for Jesus' friends to bury him. The text tells us that it was the Jewish Day of Preparation. John is thinking of the Passover festival, that celebration of a night's journey from slavery to freedom. This is what the Lord's Passover means until time ends: the journey from all that holds us captive into the glorious freedom of the children of God.

All is accomplished. And all has just begun. The next verse leaps across the chasm of death into that promised new world whose seeds are sown in this garden early on the first day of the week. So we live out our days in preparation, looking in hope for the act of God that changes everything, listening for the voice that asks us whom we are seeking and that calls us by our name.

References

Augustine (1992) *The Confessions*, tr. Henry Chadwick, Oxford: Oxford University Press.

Austin, J. L. (1962) *How To Do Things With Words*, Oxford: Clarendon Press.

Bieringer, R., Pollefeyt, D. and Vandecasteele-Vanneuville, F. (eds) (2001) *Anti-Judaism and the Fourth Gospel*, London: Westminster John Knox Press.

Bonhoeffer, Dietrich (1970) *Letters and Papers from Prison*, London: SCM Press.

Bradshaw, Peter, Review of *The Passion of the Christ*, the *Guardian*, 26 March 2004.

Brueggemann, Walter (1997) *Cadences of Home: Preaching Among Exiles*, Louisville: Westminster John Knox Press.

Corley, Kathleen E. and Webb, Robert L. (2004) *Jesus and Mel Gibson's The Passion of the Christ: The Film, the Gospels and the Claims of History*, London: Continuum.

Cragg, Kenneth (1964) *The Dome and the Rock: Jerusalem Studies in Islam*, London: SPCK.

de Rougemont, Denis (1960) *Passion and Society*, London: Faber.

Eagleton, Terry (2003) *Sweet Violence: The Idea of the Tragic*, Oxford: Blackwell.

Ecclestone, Alan (1987) *The Scaffolding of Spirit: Reflections on the Gospel of St John*, London: Darton, Longman and Todd.

Eckardt, Alice L. and Eckardt, A. Roy (1988) *Long Night's Journey Into Day: A Revised Retrospective on the Holocaust*, Detroit: Wayne State University Press.

Ellul, Jacques (1970) *Violence: Reflections from a Christian Perspective*, London: SCM Press.

Ford, David (1995) 'Constructing a Public Theology' in Frances Young (ed.) *Dare We Speak of God in Public? The Edward Cadbury Lectures, 1993–4*, London: Mowbrays.

Frey, Nancy Louise (1999) *Pilgrim Stories: On and Off the Road to Santiago – Journeys Along an Ancient Way in Modern Spain*, Berkeley and Los Angeles: University of California Press.

Gardner, Helen (1972) 'The Dream of the Rood' (tr.) in Helen Gardner (ed.) *The Faber Book of Religious Verse*, London: Faber.

Girard, René (2004) 'On Mel Gibson's *The Passion of the Christ*' on the Stanford University Anthropoetics website: <www.anthropoetics.ucla.edu/ap1001/RGGibson.htm>; tr. Robert Doran, from 'A propos du film de Mel Gibson, *La Passion du Christ*', *Le Figaro* newspaper, March 2004.

Gorringe, Tim (1994) *Alan Ecclestone: Priest as Revolutionary*, Sheffield: Cairns Publications.

Harries, Richard (2004) *The Passion in Art*, Aldershot: Ashgate.

Jowett, Benjamin (1900) *Thucydides Translated into English*, Oxford: Clarendon Press.

Kenny, Anthony (2006) *What I Believe*, London: Continuum.

Kierkegaard, Søren (1973) 'The Present Age', tr. Alexander Dru in Robert Bretall (ed.) *A Kierkegaard Anthology*, Princeton, NJ: Princeton University Press.

Lomax, Eric (1996) *The Railway Man*, London: Vintage.

McLeod, Hugh (1995) 'The Privatisation of Religion in Modern England' in Frances Young (ed.) *Dare We Speak of God in Public? The Edward Cadbury Lectures, 1993–4*, London: Mowbray.

Miller, Patrick D. (2005) 'Heaven's Prisoners: The Lament as Christian Prayer' in Sally Brown and Patrick D. Miller (eds) *Lament: Reclaiming Practices in Pulpit, Pew and Public Square*, Louisville: Westminster John Knox Press.

Minsky, Rosalind (2000) 'Consuming Goods' in Adrienne Baker (ed.) *Serious Shopping: Essays in Psychotherapy and Consumerism*, London: Free Association Books.

Moltmann, Jürgen (1974), *The Crucified God*, London: SCM Press.

Morrison, Blake (1993) *And When Did You Last See Your Father?*, London: Penguin.

—— (2003) *Things My Mother Never Told Me*, London: Vintage.

Nicholl, Donald (1997) *Triumphs of the Spirit in Russia*, London: Darton, Longman and Todd.

Orchard, Helen (1998) 'Courting Betrayal: Jesus as Victim in the Gospel of John', *Journal for the Study of the New Testament*, Supplement Series 161, Sheffield.

Paffenroth, Kim (2001) *Judas: Images of the Lost Disciple*, London: Westminster John Knox Press.

Rensberger, David (1988) *Overcoming the World: Politics and Community in the Gospel of John*, London: SPCK.

Robertson, F. W. (1903) 'The Scepticism of Pilate' in *Sermons Preached at Brighton: First Series*, London: Kegan Paul.

Ross, Ellen (1997) *The Grief of God: Images of the Suffering Jesus in Late Medieval England*, Oxford: Oxford University Press.

Sadgrove, Michael (1995) *A Picture of Faith: A Meditation on the Imagery of Christ in Glory*, Rattlesden: Kevin Mayhew.

Schweitzer, Albert (1923) *J. S. Bach*, tr. Ernest Newman, London: Black.

Sykes, Stephen (2006) *Power and Christian Theology*, London: Continuum.

Taylor, John V. (1963) *The Primal Vision*, London: SCM Press.

Vanstone, W. H. (1979) *Love's Endeavour, Love's Expense: The Response of Being to the Love of God*, London: Darton, Longman and Todd.

—— (1982) *The Stature of Waiting*, London: Darton, Longman and Todd.

Van Zeller, Dom Hubert (1959) *The Holy Rule: Notes on St Benedict's Legislation for Monks*, London: Sheed & Ward.

Wright, N. T. (1996) *Jesus and the Victory of God*, London: SPCK.

Wroe, Ann (1999) *Pilate: The Biography of an Invented Man*, London: Jonathan Cape.

Yalom, Irvin D. (1991) *Love's Executioner and Other Tales of Psychotherapy*, London: HarperCollins.

A Note on Books

In the Introduction to this book, I said that my debt to New Testament scholarship would be clear. I owe it to readers to indicate where I have found particular help, and this may suggest ideas for further reading (for other books, see the References).

My first acknowledgement must be to two monumental works of Raymond Brown: his commentary *The Gospel According to John* (1966, New York: Doubleday) and his study of the Passion Narratives *The Death of the Messiah* (1994, London: Geoffrey Chapman). These books are a mine of historical information and of theological insight.

I have frequently returned with gratitude to old favourites among the commentaries: in chronological order, John Calvin (1553), B. F. Westcott (1880), Edward Hoskyns and F. N. Davey (1947), and R. H. Lightfoot (1956). More recent commentaries include John Marsh (1968), Rudolph Bultmann (tr. 1971), Barnabas Lindars (1972), C. K. Barrett (1978), Rudolph Schnackenburg (1982), Ernst Haenchen (1984), Gerard S. Sloyan (1988), Ben Witherington III (1995), René Kiefer (in the *Oxford Bible Commentary*, 2001) and Andrew Lincoln (2005).

I should also mention other studies: C. H. Dodd, *The Interpretation of the Fourth Gospel* (1953, Cambridge: CUP), and *Historical Tradition in the Fourth Gospel* (1965, Cambridge: CUP); Stephen Smalley, *John: Evangelist and Interpreter* (1979, Exeter: Paternoster); Raymond Brown, *The Community of the Beloved Disciple* (1979, New York: Paulist Press); Kenneth Grayston, *Dying We Live: A New Enquiry into the Death of Christ in the New Testament* (1990, London: Darton, Longman and Todd); Donald, C. R. Senior, *The Passion of Jesus in the Gospel of John* (1991, Gracewing: Leominster); Mark Stibbe, *John as Storyteller: Narrative Criticism and the Fourth Gospel* (1992, Cambridge: CUP); J. Duncan M. Derrett, *The Victim: The Johannine Passion Narrative Reexamined* (1993, Shipston-on-Stour: Peter Drinkwater); William Klassen, *Judas: Betrayer or Friend of Jesus?* (1996, London: SCM) and Sandra Schneiders, *Written That You May Believe: Encountering Jesus in the Fourth Gospel* (1999, New York: Crossroad Publishing).